John McPhee

Twayne's United States Authors Series

Frank Day, Editor
Clemson University

TUSAS 674

JOHN McPHEE IN PRINCETON (1993).
Photo courtesy of Joel Mednick.

John McPhee

Michael Pearson

Old Dominion University

Twayne Publishers
An Imprint of Simon & Schuster Macmillan
New York

Prentice Hall International
London • Mexico City • New Delhi • Singapore • Sydney • Toronto

Twayne's United States Authors Series No. 674

John McPhee
Michael Pearson

Twayne Publishers
An Imprint of Simon & Schuster Macmillan
1633 Broadway
New York, NY 10019

Library of Congress Cataloging-in-Publication Data
Pearson, Michael.
    John McPhee / Michael Pearson
        p.   cm. — (Twayne's United States authors series ; TUSAS 674)
    Includes bibliographical references and index.
    ISBN 0-8057-4624-2 (alk. paper)
    1. McPhee, John A.   2. Authors, American—20th century—Biography.
  3. Journalists—United States—Biography.   I. Title.   II. Series.
CT275.M4449P43   1997
808'.0092—dc20   96-36762
  [B]   CIP

The paper used in this publication meets the minimum requirements of American
National Standard for Information Sciences—Permanence of Paper for Printed Library
Materials. ANSI Z39.48-1984. ∞ ™

10 9 8 7 6 5 4 3 2 1 (hc)

Printed in the United States of America

In memory of my father, the first craftsman I knew, and Henry W. Sams, scholar and mentor

Contents

Preface   *ix*
Acknowledgments   *xiii*
Chronology   *xv*

Chapter One
Biography   1

Chapter Two
Literary Nonfiction   11

Chapter Three
The Reporter as Artist   21

Chapter Four
The McPhee Hero   32

Chapter Five
The Experience of Place   62

Chapter Six
Science and Technology   85

Chapter Seven
Nature   100

Chapter Eight
The Shape of the Future   122

Notes and References   *129*
Selected Bibliography   *135*
Index   *141*

Preface

For over thirty years John McPhee, a staff writer for the *New Yorker,* has pleased both readers and critics with his taut prose, at once detailed and restrained, and his richly textured narratives on subjects ranging from the commonplace to the exotic. As much as any writer in the past quarter of a century, McPhee has helped establish the literary credibility of nonfiction writing. For many years scholars and critics seemed to consider nonfiction writing to be synonymous with daily journalism and therefore, in their minds, ephemeral, but in the mid-1960s McPhee, along with writers like Truman Capote and Gay Talese, began to demonstrate some of the aesthetic possibilities of the form. Because of his prolificacy and the consistent quality of his books, McPhee, perhaps more than any other nonfiction writer of his generation, has legitimized the literary importance of nonfiction. In 1987 *The Harper American Literature* anthology included an excerpt from McPhee's 1977 bestseller *Coming into the Country,* and the anthology editor said, "Published in book form, his work documents his insatiable curiosity about what is extraordinary in the ordinary world."[1]

McPhee's acceptance by the literary establishment is well deserved. He has written twenty-three books, masterful accounts of people and places, a body of work unvarying in excellence. It is appropriate that the Harper anthology embraced his work, for it belongs alongside that of Alice Walker and Raymond Carver, Bobbie Ann Mason and John Updike, Dave Smith and Charles Wright—beside his respected contemporaries, regardless of their chosen genre.

In the 1960s, when McPhee began his career in literary nonfiction, the cauldron of the Vietnam War seethed, and drugs and despair seemed to shape a new, confusing world—one in which the very capacity to feel wonder appeared to be threatened. The nonfiction of Norman Mailer, Joan Didion, and Tom Wolfe mirrored this sense of chaos and exhaustion. In such a context, McPhee's work may seem to be an anomaly, but in an important respect, it too was a reflection of the times. His stories often offer pastoral images of place and portray self-reliant, independent figures. But the places and the people are usually on the edges of our culture—loners in the New Jersey Pine Barrens, fruit pickers in Florida orange groves, merchant seamen separated from their families, trappers in the wilds of Alaska, geologists roaming the basins and ranges of the West. These characters are marginal, but they are, typically, not lost. Rather, they are heroes on the margins of American life, men and women who have a clear sense of where they are and what is important to them. In a world in which the existential malaise seems a part of the air we breathe, McPhee is drawn to places that are quiet and still and to people with a moral vision. He is drawn to places that seem to hold time at bay—an island off the coast of Scotland, an oasis amidst the megalopolis, the solitude of the mountains, the sea, the rivers. He is attracted to men and women of skill and commitment—artisans, scientists, environmentalists, athletes, doctors.

With the same grace and subtlety that Willa Cather possessed, McPhee is a storyteller and only by implication do his narratives, with their ordinary heroes and pastoral images, make a cultural criticism. He is the best of our peripatetic writers, venturing out into the worlds we might never see and reminding us of the worlds right before our eyes that have been lost to us through inattention or dull habit. He is a traveler, but there is a stillness in his work, a humanity in his narratives that seems fixed and unshakable. He has employed the techniques of the fiction writer to make art of his journalism, but he has remained faithful in his obligation to fact. In each of his books he has managed to be artful without ever crossing the line into fiction. For a new generation of literary journalists, his work is the standard that they must strive for in their own writing.

In order to approach writing about McPhee's prodigious body of work, I felt that it was necessary to lift the books out of their chronology and discuss them in terms of their thematic similarities. Therefore, there is a chapter on the McPhee hero, which discusses his developing sense of the profile form and the type of individual he typically writes about. There are chapters on his books that deal with nature, with science and technology, and those that seem to emphasize his attitudes toward place. The subjects McPhee chooses to write about are intimately connected to the story of his early life; therefore, this study opens with a biographical section that serves as an aperture through which his career can be viewed. The second chapter, which briefly describes the evolution of literary nonfiction, places McPhee's writing in a necessary historical context. The chapter entitled "The Reporter as Artist" focuses on the methods and techniques that separate his work from the ordinary journalist's.

I have been fortunate in this study to have had the opportunity to interview John McPhee on a number of occasions over the past few years. For a man reputed to be reclusive, he was generous with his time, always amiable and informative, answering questions, drawing maps on the backs of cocktail napkins, acting as tour guide around the town of Princeton. I have also had the occasion to interview a number of other literary journalists while working on this book, and in the concluding chapter I incorporated their insights about McPhee into my interpretation of his achievement, an accomplishment that goes beyond journalism into the domain of literature.

Acknowledgments

I would like to express my appreciation to Old Dominion University for leave time to write this book and to Elaine Dawson for her word-processing genius, which always came with a smile. I also owe a debt to the writers of nonfiction—Walt Harrington, Mark Singer, Mark Kramer, Mike D'Orso, and Lee Gutkind—who spoke with me about McPhee's work. But my biggest debt is to John McPhee himself, for meeting with me on a number of occasions but even more importantly for the books he has written.

Chronology

1931 John Angus McPhee is born on 8 March, in Princeton, New Jersey.

1937–1951 Spends the summer months at Keewaydin Camp in Vermont.

1948 Graduates from Princeton High School and enters Deerfield Academy in Massachusetts.

1949 Enters Princeton University.

1952 Publishes his first piece of professional writing in the *New York Times Magazine*.

1953 Graduates from Princeton University after writing a novel, *Skimmer Burns,* as his undergraduate thesis.

1953–1954 Spends a year doing postgraduate study at Cambridge University in England.

1955–1956 Writes television scripts for "Robert Montgomery Presents."

1957 Begins work as a reporter for *Time* magazine.

1963 "Basketball and Beefeaters" appears—his first story to be sold to the *New Yorker.*

1965 His first book, *A Sense of Where You Are,* based on a profile of the basketball player Bill Bradley that appeared in the *New Yorker,* is published by Farrar, Straus and Giroux, who will publish all of his succeeding books. In the same year, he becomes a staff writer for the *New Yorker.*

1966 *The Headmaster.*

1967 *Oranges.*

1968 *The Pine Barrens; A Roomful of Hovings and Other Profiles.*

1969 *Levels of the Game.*

1970   *The Crofter and the Laird.*

1971   *Encounters with the Archdruid.*

1973   *The Deltoid Pumpkin Seed.*

1974   *The Curve of Binding Energy.*

1975   *Pieces of the Frame; The Survival of the Bark Canoe.*

1976   *The John McPhee Reader,* a collection edited by William Howarth.

1977   *Coming into the Country;* Award in Literature from the American Academy and Institute of Arts and Letters.

1979   *Giving Good Weight.*

1981   *Basin and Range.*

1982   Woodrow Wilson Award from Princeton University; American Association of Petroleum Geologists Journalism Award.

1983   *In Suspect Terrain.*

1984   *La Place de la Concorde Suisse.*

1985   *Table of Contents.*

1986   *Rising from the Plains.*

1989   *The Control of Nature.*

1990   *Looking for a Ship.*

1993   *Assembling California.*

1994   *The Ransom of Russian Art.*

1996   The second *John McPhee Reader,* a collection edited by Patricia Strachnan with an introduction by David Remnick.

Chapter One

Biography

Background and Early Life

When John Angus McPhee was born in Princeton, New Jersey, on 8 March 1931, in the heart of the Depression and in a state that was already on its way to gaining a reputation for soot and suburbs, it was a quaint town of about seven thousand. It hasn't changed too drastically in the more than half a century that he has lived there. It is still a town that appears to balance the bucolic and the intellectual gracefully. Now there are over thirty thousand residents, and the university enrolls nearly seven thousand students. But the streets are still dappled with leaves in the fall and shaded by old sycamores and oaks in the summertime. The town of Princeton may be only a few minutes from Trenton and a brief train ride from Philadelphia or New York City, but it still seems light years away from urban blight and smog-filled roads.

William Howarth, the editor of *The John McPhee Reader*, said of McPhee that Princeton is "the epicenter of his cartography."[1] In many respects the town of Princeton does serve as the foundation for his work. His, it seems, was an idyllic boyhood, and in subtle ways his writing reflects that upbringing. Except for a year at Deerfield Academy, another at Cambridge University, and a few years in New York City, McPhee has spent his entire life in Princeton. Most of the topics he has written about are a reflection, perhaps, of his Princeton roots, of an orderly universe populated by men and women of skill, intelligence, and varied interests, the same type of characters who appear in his books. The personality of the town of Princeton, according to William Howarth, is multifarious and particularly American, and surely McPhee's work describes archetypal American characters—independent, hopeful, active, capable. For McPhee the town has "a great many strands in the braid—it can't be easily characterized."[2] Neither can McPhee's books, on subjects that range from oranges to the Swiss army. But McPhee's calm, ordered prose, the hallmark of his stories, may be a reflection of the elegant stability that he has experienced over the years in Princeton, a place that has provided him with a point of departure for his journalistic forays into the world around him.

McPhee's father, Harry Roemer McPhee, a general practitioner with an interest in sports medicine and a physician for the U.S. Olympic teams and Princeton athletic squads for over a quarter of a century, was born in 1895. McPhee's paternal grandfather, Angus, was a heater in a steel mill in the Midwest, a worker whose job it was to get the ingots fiery hot before they went on to the roller. McPhee's great-grandfather was a Scotsman, a Highlander who married a young woman from the Lowlands in 1858 on his way to work in the mines of Ohio. According to McPhee this adventurous Scotsman "has about a hundred and thirty descendants who have sprayed out into the American milieu, and they have included railroad engineers, railroad conductors, brakemen, firemen, steelworkers, teachers, football coaches, a chemist, a chemical engineer, a policeman, a grocer, salesmen."[3] And, of course, there was a doctor, McPhee's father, who moved from Iowa State University to Princeton shortly before John, his youngest child, was born. McPhee's older siblings, his brother Roemer and his sister Laura Anne, were born in Iowa. McPhee's mother, Mary Ziegler, had been a teacher in Cleveland.

The family bought a house at 21 Maple Street, which was then on the edge of the town of Princeton and not far from farms and woods. The house was within an easy bike ride or walk to campus, and McPhee, who was passionate about sports, spent much of his time at the football practice fields on Olden Street or in the gym during basketball season. Because his father was in sports medicine, the young McPhee didn't have much trouble sneaking into the gym with other professors' sons to shoot baskets or getting a job retrieving field-goal attempts at Princeton University football games. "I spent so much time playing sports," McPhee once said, "that I sometimes wonder how I ever got any work done in school" (Personal Interview).

Somehow he managed to do quite well, although he claims to have "flunked kindergarten." He did spend two years preparing for first grade, but he skipped a grade in elementary school and graduated from Princeton High School soon after his seventeenth birthday. Princeton Elementary School on Nassau Street, which he attended for eight years, was not far from his home, and now, fittingly perhaps, it is the facility for the university's creative writing program, in which McPhee teaches a course on nonfiction literature.

McPhee's years at Princeton High School were formative ones for him as a writer. He was still active in sports—a canoeist, a tennis player, captain of the basketball team—but he also made the acquaintance of

Olive McKee during that time. She was his English teacher for three years and proved to be one of the most demanding editors he would encounter in his writing career. Each week she assigned three compositions. Students had to hand in a detailed structural outline with each piece of writing, and frequently the students had to read their essays in front of the class. Today McPhee's books are renowned for the purity of the prose and the subtlety of structure. He reads every sentence of each of his books aloud to his wife before it is published, and each book is organized, it seems, by a man who loves to find the right pattern in events and outline it. Remembering Ms. McKee, he has said, "I feel a large and considerable debt to her."[4]

After graduating from Princeton High, McPhee wanted to go straight to college, but his mother thought that he needed more time to mature. As McPhee recently said, "She was firm, and in that sort of situation you *listened* to her" (Personal Interview). McPhee went to Deerfield Academy for a year, studying under the general guidance of Frank L. Boyden, a man he later immortalized in *The Headmaster*. In that book he described Boyden as "an educator by intuition . . . one of the great headmasters in history, and for many years he has stood alone as, in all probability, the last man of his kind" (*Headmaster*, 7). At Deerfield, McPhee met some of his most influential teachers and mentors. Besides Frank Boyden, there was his wife, Helen, who taught chemistry; Frank Conklin, who taught geology; and Robert McGlynn, who taught English and sparked in McPhee a deeper love of reading than he had ever experienced. The school itself must surely be described as one of the most serene and pastoral educational institutions in the United States. McPhee does not overstate the case when he writes, "It would be difficult to imagine a more beautiful setting for a school or a more attractive school in the setting" (9). It must have been a paradise for a young man with a quick, active mind who was enthusiastic about sports and interested in the natural world. The quiet street that runs past the Academy still has farmhouses and barns. The school sits on a knoll consisting of over a hundred acres of ivy-covered buildings and manicured playing fields. In many respects, Deerfield seems to be a separate universe, only inconsequentially touched by the modern world. Such places, filled with people who were seemingly out of step with contemporary society, became the subject of many of McPhee's stories.

In 1949 McPhee entered Princeton University, where he played basketball on the freshman team, wrote for the college literary magazines, and eventually convinced the rather conservative English Department to accept his novel, *Skimmer Burns,* for the required senior thesis. During his four years in college McPhee was also a regular contestant on a weekly radio and television program called "Twenty Questions," a show in which individuals on a panel must guess a mystery item by asking yes or no questions. Clearly, this experience was groundwork for a man who became famous for writing on all manner of animals, vegetables, and minerals during his career. William Howarth saw the media experience as particularly useful for the budding nonfiction writer: "The training was probably useful for a future journalist; it taught him how to assemble facts and infer their hidden meanings."[5] At five feet seven inches tall, McPhee may have sensed the limits of his basketball career, but he had decided at an early age that he wanted to be a writer and by the age of eighteen that he wanted to write for the *New Yorker.* Therefore, one of his most important activities while at Princeton University was his writing for the school publications—the *Nassau Sovereign,* the *Princeton Tiger,* and the *Nassau Literary Magazine.* When McPhee became editor of the *Princeton Tiger,* the school's humor magazine, in the spring of his junior year and the fall of his senior year, he consciously tried to imitate the form and style of the *New Yorker.* He might have sensed that he was on the right track when an editor from the *New York Times Magazine* asked him to write an article about college humor magazines, and he had his first piece of professional writing published in 1952, at the age of twenty-one. In his senior year he wrote regular fact pieces for the *Princeton Alumni Weekly* in a column titled "On the Campus."

After receiving his B.A. in English from Princeton in 1953, he spent a year at Cambridge University in England, studying literature and in his spare time touring the Midlands to play basketball against teams from Oxford or the London School of Economics. His first essay to be accepted by the *New Yorker,* "Basketball and Beefeaters," published in 1963, recounts his experiences playing on the Cambridge team against the Royal Fusiliers in a game that was scheduled to be in the Tower of London. While in England he also worked as a stringer for *Time* magazine.

McPhee's experiences working as a stringer while in England, his years on the Princeton University magazines, his time at Deerfield, or even his tutelage under the guidance of Olive McKee were all important in shaping him as a writer, but there was one other experience that dominated his youth and that helped form his vision of the world around him. Keewaydin, a camp for boys on the shores of Lake Dunmore about ten miles south of Middlebury, Vermont, influenced his interests and choice of subjects to write about as much as anything else in his life. In a recent conversation with me he said, "A few years back I was giving a talk at Vassar and a young man raised his hand and asked me what academic institution had influenced me the most. Well, I had gone to Princeton High School and Princeton University and Cambridge, but I didn't hesitate for a second. I said Keewaydin; it was a real educational institution. I started going there when I was six and I was working as a camp counselor when I was in college" (Personal Interview).

Camp Keewaydin fans out along a bay at one end of Lake Dunmore. The camp has five hundred acres of hiking trails and mountain inclines, and the main section of the camp sits quietly in the bowl created by the Green Mountains. The camp director, Alfred Hare, Jr., known to everyone associated with Keewaydin as Waboos, remembers Johnny McPhee quite well. "He was an outstanding camper and a superior staff person," Hare recalled recently. "He was the best writer we ever had for the camp newspaper, *The Kicker.* He had a wonderful sense of humor. He dressed those stories up in his special style and read them with great dramatic flair. Right here may have just been where he got his start in the sort of literary journalism that he does so well now."[6] In a letter addressed to Waboos on 9 August 1972, McPhee pointed to the debt he felt he owed Keewaydin as a writer. "So much of the work I do derives from interests developed at Keewaydin that I have come to think of a number of my books as 'the Keewaydin stories'[,] . . . *Encounters with the Archdruid* and *The Pine Barrens* are probably first among the group, for they are thematically tied quite closely to Keewaydin and they are rooted in attitudes acquired there. They involve canoe trips and wild rides through rapids and backpacking walks in wilderness."[7] In that same letter, McPhee goes on to say that even though he did not learn how to play basketball in the wilderness setting of Camp Keewaydin, he was involved in "some whimsical flurries of the game" and he did learn to play tennis there. "The level where I loved tennis the most," McPhee writes, "was there by the ice house."

Keewaydin is a place where McPhee's love of sports was encouraged and nurtured. It was also a place where his love of the natural world developed. If a whaling ship was Melville's Harvard and Yale, Keewaydin may have been McPhee's. Of course, he had Princeton and Cambridge, too. After his year at Cambridge, McPhee knew that he wanted to become a writer, but he had yet to figure out exactly what kind of a writer he wanted to be. As he said in an interview with Norman Sims, "Being out of school at last and knowing you never wanted to do anything but be a writer is a perplexing time in life. Saying you want to be a writer isn't the same as being in a training program as an investment broker or something tangible. How the hell do you become a writer? What do you do?"[8]

Discovering His Vocation

McPhee came back to the United States and lived in New York for a time while he tried his hand at freelancing and attempted unsuccessfully to get his novel *Skimmer Burns* published. The novel, which was dedicated to Robert McGlynn, an English teacher at Deerfield, demonstrates most of the signs of a young writer searching for a medium. Often it is amateurish and heavy handed, but it also has interesting autobiographical resonances. The main character, Duncan "Skimmer" Burns, stars on a television quiz show while he is in college. The show, which has far more than a passing resemblance to "Twenty Questions," focuses the readers' attention on the protagonist's main problem, figuring out how best to live his life and what best to do with it—teach, act, write. Interestingly, the novel begins and ends with the image of a canoe, the idea that "a canoe points in two directions." For the canoeist and for the beginning writer, caught perhaps between writing fact and fiction, this must have been a significant symbol. As an early piece of writing, it does not show too much of McPhee's later brilliance, but it surely is competent and, in addition, shows some of the hallmarks of his later writing. For instance, there is a hint of Olive McKee's influence in the work of fiction. The novel has three sections to it, echoing Ms. McKee's three-part compositions. There is also a lengthy appendix in which the Princeton senior outlines his structural and thematic intentions and emphasizes his interest in character over philosophizing or argument (as McPhee wrote in the appendix—"make characters, not caricatures, individuals, not types").

McPhee was eighteen when he decided that he wanted one day to write for the *New Yorker*. His dream was to write a long fact piece, but it took fourteen years and an imposing collection of rejection slips before the magazine published "Basketball and Beefeaters" when he was thirty-two. But during those fourteen years he didn't merely wait for the *New Yorker* to answer his call. As an apprentice writer, he tried his hand at all aspects of the craft. "I didn't rule out anything as a younger writer," he has said. "I tried everything, sometimes with hilarious results. I think that young writers have to roll around like oranges on a conveyor belt. They have to try it all" (Personal Interview). True to this statement, McPhee, as a young writer, tried his hand at fiction and drama, as well as journalism. A short stint in the business world, writing speeches for executives and articles for company publications at W. R. Grace and Company in New York City, taught him that he was not cut out to be a corporate man. In his short story "Eucalyptus Trees," published in 1967, he may have been making this point dramatically. In the story, the main character, Ian Gibbons, resigns his position in a company because the managers refuse to give him a transfer that would make it possible for him to see the eucalyptus trees that he has been writing about for them. "It's nothing personal," they tell him, but for Gibbons and McPhee, as well, the "individual case" is ultimately always the important issue.[9]

Even though he was not able to sell *Skimmer Burns* and his primary goal was to write nonfiction, McPhee continued to write some fiction during his early years as a professional writer. During those years his interest in fiction waned as his fascination with nonfiction swelled. As late as 1968, however, he was still writing short stories, publishing "Ruth, the Sun is Shining" in *Playboy*. The story begins with the description of a character named Bobby Norton who is lecturing his wife about heat lightning, saying that there is no such thing. Soon after the opening scene the narrator explains that Norton "never needed much of an occasion for one of these lectures. If he had the information, it would eventually come out; and he was full of information."[10] At the end of the story Norton disappears in a burst of smoke and sound, the victim of his own misinterpretation of the facts. This may have been McPhee's parabolic warning to himself. During the next 25 years McPhee would become a master of telling a story filled with information without ever appearing to lecture his readers and without ever being imprecise with his facts. Unlike Norton, McPhee seems to relish not the facts but what they can tell his readers about character and situation. In an interview with Douglas Vipond and Russell Hunt in 1991, McPhee said, "That's the common denominator of all the work I've done and that's what attracts me to it. I'm describing people engaged in their thing, their activity, whatever it is. . . . I find myself disappointed when I read something like 'This writer is really interested in *facts,* he just loves *facts*.' It's like saying that somebody who is a painter really loves *paint,* he just can't get enough of it, he eats it in the morning."[11] For McPhee the facts are his materials, but the story is his object. By the early 1960s McPhee was already revising the fiction writer's dictum of "show, don't tell" into "show *and* tell." Pamela Marsh recognized this skill when she wrote in the *Christian Science Monitor,* "John McPhee ought to be a bore. He has all the qualifications. With a bore's persistence he seizes a subject, shakes loose a cloud of more detail than we ever imagined we could care to hear on any subject—yet somehow he makes the whole procedure curiously fascinating."[12]

For a few years as a freelance writer McPhee wrote, among other things, television scripts for "Robert Montgomery Presents." He wrote five scripts, NBC bought three, and two of them ("In a Foreign City" and "The Man Who Vanished"), based on *New Yorker* stories written by Robert Coates, were produced. There were pleasures for the young writer in writing such scripts, mainly crafting the dialogue, but overall it was frustrating because, as McPhee once said, "I didn't have the impression that I was making the whole shoe" (Personal Interview). In 1957 he became a reporter for *Time,* writing for the "Show Business" section and producing profiles of celebrities such as Jackie Gleason, Sophia Loren, Barbra Streisand, Richard Burton, and Joan Baez. Eventually he was promoted to associate editor, but none of these successes made him forget his first dream: to become a *New Yorker* writer.

A *New Yorker* Staff Writer

"In 1963" the story McPhee had originally written for an editor at *Esquire,* where it was rejected, ended up in the 16 March issue of the *New Yorker.* "Basketball and Beefeaters" is a short, softly ironic essay that tells a sports tale one might expect to hear from Ring Lardner if he had been edited by E. B. White. With gentle good humor, McPhee describes his experiences playing basketball for Cambridge University in a gymnasium that was in a building called the Department of Human Ecology. In their own gym this Cambridge team, made up of three Americans, a few Britons, a Scotsman, a young man from Trinidad and another from the Phillippines, were virtually unconquerable, but on the road it was a different story, for it seems each team had an idiosyncratic gymnasium. The Cambridge gym was unique because it was the smallest one around. As McPhee writes, "It was possible, though rarely attempted, to complete a solo fast break from one end of the court to the other with a single high-parabola dribble" ("Beefeaters," in *Pieces of the Frame,* 145). But the story is really about playing basketball, or nearly playing it, in the Tower of London against Her Majesty's Royal Fusiliers. Because of an unfortunate accident the game had to be played in a sports hall nearby, but for McPhee the game was a genuine victory. Cambridge won by fifty-three points, a modern "beheading," as he says, but more important, his recollection of the event opened to him the door to the *New Yorker.* By January 1965 McPhee had left his job at *Time* and was concentrating his full energy on becoming part of the *New Yorker* staff. In 1965 he got his chance with an in-depth profile of the Princeton all-American basketball player Bill Bradley.

In the winter of 1962 McPhee had received a call from his father, a notoriously taciturn fan of Princeton teams and a former college basketball player. He told McPhee to come down from New York City to watch a player he described with unaccustomed effusiveness as "the best basketball player who has ever been near here and may be one of the best ever" (*A Sense of Where You Are,* 4). What McPhee found was "the most graceful and classical player who had ever been near Princeton, to say the very least" (*Sense,* 5). McPhee decided to write about Bradley after the Princeton–St. Joseph's game in the national tournament in 1963. Soon after the story appeared in the *New Yorker* Bradley led his team to the final four of the NCAA championships, had broken Oscar Robertson's record by scoring fifty-eight points against Wichita in the consolation game, had been named the most valuable player of the tournament, and had been selected as the first pick in the NBA draft.

After "A Sense of Where You Are" appeared in the *New Yorker,* McPhee was made a staff writer at the magazine. (The article was published as a book of the same name.) William Howarth has referred to McPhee's position as "one of the most liberated jobs in modern journalism."[13] McPhee has tried to modify this perception, however, by explaining that he doesn't get a salary but rather is paid only for what the *New Yorker* publishes. At the end of the year, he gets a 1099 form, not a W-2. A man devoted to his family (his wife Yolanda and his four daughters from his first marriage and four stepchildren), McPhee may have felt the pressure to publish or perish more sharply than the academics that surround him in Princeton. His books are often dedicated to his family, pictures of them fill his office, and although he is not always willing to talk about his private life, he always seems ready to speak about his daughters' accomplishments—Martha's first novel, Martha and Jenny's translation of the Pope's best-selling book from Italian into English, Sarah's first full-time teaching job as a professor at Emory University, or Laura's work as a professor of photography in Massachusetts.

During his three decades of work for the *New Yorker,* McPhee has written twenty-three books on a kaleidoscopic range of topics, everything from canoes and oranges to tennis and nuclear energy. Along the way, he has made a reputation for himself as a meticulous and ethical observer, a profoundly skillful stylist, a master of complex organization, a storyteller of the first order. McPhee is recognized by many critics as one of the premier living writers of literary nonfiction. As one critic, Ronald Weber, phrased it, McPhee has the ability in his work to go beyond "the flow of fact—as engrossing as that is in itself—to endow fact with both coherence and the odd resonance that belongs to a work of art."[14]

Chapter Two
Literary Nonfiction

The Origins of Literary Nonfiction

The genre of literary nonfiction is relatively new. Essentially it is a form of writing that began to flourish in the early 1960s, around the time McPhee began publishing his books, and that has become increasingly popular and respected since then. Some would go so far as to say, as Theodore A. Rees Cheney does, that "Nonfiction is, indeed, the new American literature."[1] In *The Literature of Fact* Ronald Weber attempts to account for the contemporary appeal of literary nonfiction, the sizable audiences attracted to Mailer, Wolfe, Talese, Capote, McPhee, Didion, and others. As Weber explains the phenomenon, some theorists feel that political and social dislocations have caused contemporary readers to find it easier to engage with nonfiction. Others feel that the idea of the practicality of nonfiction appeals to an impatient modern audience. Timeliness gave the form a special edge, a way of confronting a rapidly changing and confusing reality. Weber says that another way of accounting for the popularity of the form is that it is an I writing for an I, "personal writing for an age of personalism." For some, it was a form of writing that, by its very nature, challenged consensual wisdom and accepted authority. For others, it was a response to the "emergence of a new kind of mass audience . . . a liberally educated public." It was a public that wanted to have its literature and its sense of reality, too, but much contemporary fiction suggested that reality was not definable. Therefore, perhaps, literary nonfiction was offering readers what much fiction had stopped offering them—a sense that the world, however confusing, can be represented to them. "With the new nonfiction," Weber says, "the audience received information but received it entertainingly, with familiar literary trimmings. It received an up-to-date factual fiction that abandoned the dreariness of day-to-day journalism yet did not fly off in the strange and complex ways of Barth, Borges, Barthelme, and other fabulists."[2]

Literary nonfiction has a history, though, a heritage that, although not as formal or discernible as some forms of poetry and fiction, extends back to the eighteenth century and even earlier, perhaps. Depending on how one defines the form, many early works might fit under the general heading "literary nonfiction"—St. Augustine's *Confessions,* some of Montaigne's essays, or some periodical pieces by Addison and Steele. But calling these works literary nonfiction might be the same as calling *The Canterbury Tales* a picaresque novel, a bit too much of a semantic stretch. Possibly, as some critics suggest, the form of literary nonfiction began to emerge with Daniel Defoe's *A Journal of the Plague Year,* which appeared in 1722. How much of the work is fiction and how much is fact has not been fully established, but it is clear that, as Joseph M. Webb has said, Defoe wrote the book from "a journalistic vantage point."[3] In writing about the great plague that struck London in 1665, Defoe could have pulled some of the information for the book from his memory of the events (although he was only five years old at the time) and some could have been gleaned from interviews and books. *A Journal* has the feel and aura of history and memoir to it. It is filled with facts and statistics, but as Louis Landa asserts in an introduction to the work, "Though history is used to authenticate the narrative, the *Journal* is essentially a work of the imagination, a reshaping of a voluminous body of fact, embellished and ascribed to a single individual who, even if he has a historical prototype, is still fictional as presented in the pattern of actions, motives, and thoughts, the whole selected and arranged to achieve certain effects and to suggest certain truths about helpless man as he rolls 'darkling down the torrent of his fate.' "[4]

As the novel rose in popularity in the eighteenth century with Fielding, Richardson, and Defoe, so did the appeal of true narratives. Novelists created forms—the epistolary novel or the picaresque story—that imitated nonfiction patterns. Writers published their diaries and their accounts of voyage and adventure. Pedro de Casteneda, Richard Hakluyt, and John Smith were travel writers who opened literary paths for others like William Least Heat-Moon, Ian Frazier, and Bruce Chatwin centuries later. James Boswell's *Life of Samuel Johnson,* published in 1791, could have served as a model for much of the immersion reporting employed by Gay Talese and John McPhee. Fiction writers like Washington Irving and Herman Melville in the nineteenth century crossed over between fiction and nonfiction when they felt the need, and some writers, like Thoreau and Emerson, focused primarily on nonfiction. Two of Twain's most important works—*Life on the Mississippi* and *Roughing It*—are books that could be termed literary nonfiction.

The Other Literature

One of the difficulties in determining the sources of the form, in finding the literary forebears, for instance, of a John McPhee, is that until recently the genre of literary nonfiction went undefined. As William Howarth pointed out in 1976 in his introduction to *The John McPhee Reader,* volumes of McPhee's work are scattered all over the library, under call numbers for Recreation, Military Science, Education, Nature, and elsewhere. "No one," as Howarth says, "has a proper name for his brand of factual writing."[5]

In recent years, however, a number of critics have attempted to define the possibilities and boundaries of the form, making it a bit easier to trace the literary lineage of writers like McPhee. Of course, that doesn't mean that there is absolute agreement among scholars concerning the nature, limits, and effects of literary nonfiction. In 1981 John Hellman called it "a contemporary genre in which journalistic material is presented in the forms of fiction."[6] Hellman argues that all human perception and communication shape experience; therefore, when journalists select, transform, and interpret experience, they are, in a sense, creating a fiction. David Lodge seems to agree when he says in *The Novelist at the Crossroads,* "The nonfiction novel and fabulation are radical forms which take their impetus from an extreme reaction to the world we live in—*The Armies of the Night* and *Giles Goat-Boy* are equally products of the apocalyptic imagination."[7] Mas'ud Zavarzadeh sees literary nonfiction as having "the shapeliness of fiction and the authority of reality."[8] For Chris Anderson such nonfiction is "more than informative: it is an effort to persuade us to attitudes, interpretations, opinions, even actions."[9] Thomas Connery calls literary nonfiction "a third way to tell a story," another way of ordering reality that is not fiction and not strictly journalism.[10] W. Ross Winterowd argues that, even though we often associate literature with poetry and fiction, much nonfiction should be seen as "the other literature."[11]

It is this "other" literature that caused so much controversy in the mid-1960s with the publication of Truman Capote's *In Cold Blood* and Tom Wolfe's declaration that the "New Journalism" would oust the novel from its position of importance. The debate over the aesthetic and epistemological possibilities of literary nonfiction raged during the 1960s, opening up what Barbara Lounsberry called "the great unexplored territory of contemporary criticism."[12] In her introduction to *The Art of Fact,* Lounsberry summarizes what she believes are the essential features of the form: documentable subject matter, exhaustive research, use of narrative scenes, and a literary prose style.[13] Tom Wolfe, in his disputatious introduction to the anthology *The New Journalism,* mentions some of the same characteristics that Lounsberry focuses upon. After mentioning the journalists' discovery that it "just might be possible to write journalism that would . . . read like a novel," Wolfe explains how it was possible to write "accurate non-fiction with the techniques usually associated with novels and short stories."[14] Wolfe says that the basic element in creative nonfiction was scene-by-scene construction of the narrative. "Hence," Wolfe says, "the sometimes extraordinary feats of reporting that the new journalists undertook: so that they could actually witness the scenes in other people's lives as they took place." This approach allowed these writers to fulfill Wolfe's second commandment—"to record the dialogue in full." Wolfe's third essential device was the use of the third-person point of view. In this way the journalist could give the reader the feeling of being inside a given character's mind. Wolfe's fourth key is the use of symbolic details—the recording of ordinary gestures, customs, habits—in such a way that it enhances the realism of the story.

Literary journalists seek some way of suggesting a truth beyond the facts without ever altering the facts. Gay Talese suggests this when he says, "You have to know your people very, very well. And you have to be able to work within their words, and work within the framework of their lives. But if you dig deeply enough into their lives, you come up with so much that it gives a lot to work with, and you can still be creative and selective in what you choose to work with."[15] For the best writers of creative nonfiction, there must be a perfect balance of creativity and honest reporting. Norman Sims, in his first anthology of literary journalism, discussed six characteristics of the form. Such writing, he said, demands "immersion in complex, difficult subjects."[16] The writer must be willing to spend weeks, months, and sometimes years on a subject that simply might not turn out. This is a risk inherent in this type of writing. Second, these nonfiction writers must hold accuracy as one of their ultimate goals. Third, the narrative must allow for complexity and contradiction, reflecting the entangled quality of real life. Fourth, these writers must speak in a personal, unique voice, not in the institutional tones of a newspaper. Fifth, the writer has a responsibility to both his subject and to the truth. Finally, Sims focuses on a concept that he calls "The Masks of Men," what Richard Rhodes refers to as symbolic realities, the meaning of a story showing itself through specific, connotative details. In a more recent anthology, Mark Kramer and Sims add a few subtleties to the definition of the genre.[17] Literary journalism, they say, addresses the lives of ordinary men and women and emphasizes everyday occurrences. Accurately, Sims says that the classics of the genre such as James Agee's *Let Us Now Praise Famous Men* or John Hersey's *Hiroshima* "deal with the feelings and experiences of commoners."[18] Most of these writers chronicle what Susan Orlean refers to as "the dignity of ordinariness." As Tracy Kidder says, "The point is to write as well as George Eliot in *Middlemarch* and to find ways to do that in nonfiction."[19] In his essay, "Breakable Rules for Literary Journalists," Mark Kramer reiterates many of the same ideas and underscores the significance of research, the importance of using an intimate voice, and the value of a subtle structure. As Kramer sees it, there is something inherently democratic about literary journalism, "something pluralistic, pro-individual, anti-cant, and anti-elite. . . . Informal style cuts through the obfuscating generalities of creeds, countries, companies, bureaucracies, and experts. And narratives of the felt lives of everyday people test idealizations against actualities. Truth is in the details of real lives."[20]

The creativity in literary nonfiction for John McPhee and most of the other artists working in the form comes not in making things up but in sensitive, dedicated reporting and in a careful structuring of the body of information that they accumulate in the process of collecting material. This is what Joseph Mitchell was referring to when he discussed the writing of *Joe Gould's Secret:* "Everything in the Gould book is documented. . . . But I could have used this documentation in a different way. The creative aspect of it is the particularity of the facts that you choose, and the particularity of the conversations that you choose, and the fact that you stayed with the man long enough to get a panoply of conversations from which you can choose the ones that you decide are the most significant. The Gould I described, I think, is the absolutely true Gould. But another person could have written the story about Joe Gould far differently."[21] In a similar vein, this may be what Hugh Kenner is alluding to in his article in the New York Times Book Review in 1985 when he said about nonfiction writers, "You get yourself trusted by artifice."[22] All writing involves some degree of calculation, and writing that appears to be the most natural is often the most craftily calculated. Artful writing, as Wordsworth made clear, is emotion *but* it is recollected in tranquility. A nonfiction book like *Walden,* for instance, took more than five years and a number of revisions before Thoreau had his *spontaneous* masterpiece.

Modern Nonfiction

Although writers like Stephen Crane did make advances in journalism in the nineteenth century, it was rare to see Thoreau's level of literary craftsmanship in nonfiction until the 1930s, when *New Yorker* writers such as Joseph Mitchell, A. J. Liebling, and E. B White added a new voice, it seemed, to journalistic writing. Mitchell, in particular, wrote a brand of nonfiction that seemed vital and new. He wrote about the denizens of the Bowery, those who gathered in McSorley's Saloon, the people who spent their days along the wharves and in the fish markets of lower Manhattan. He wrote with great care, "meticulously assembling his stories with infinite patience."[23] A great symbolist, Mitchell looked more to James Joyce than to his fellow journalists for ways to develop his characters and themes. The famous *New Yorker* fact story, the profiles and far-flung correspondence, lifted nonfiction to the realm of art. On 31 August 1946, the *New Yorker* made an even more radical departure by printing an issue with advertisements and a weekly calendar but only one story, John Hersey's "Hiroshima," a 31,347-word account of how the bombing affected six residents of the city. Soon after, it was published in book form and did as much as any work up until that time, perhaps, to define the potential popularity and the aesthetic possibilities of literary nonfiction.

Five years before the publication of *Hiroshima*, James Agee published *Let Us Now Praise Famous Men*, a work of nonfiction about sharecroppers in the American South that stretched the limits of form and demonstrated the level of mystery that literary journalism can evoke. And a few years before Agee's *Famous Men*, George Orwell wrote a group of books—*Down and Out in Paris and London, Homage to Catalonia*, and *The Road to Wigan Pier*—that showed dramatically that nonfiction could use dialogue, scenes, point of view, and theme with exquisite balance and in a powerfully clear style. Orwell, Agee, Mitchell, Hersey and others, then, led to the flowering of literary nonfiction in the 1960s and 1970s. But 1965 may be the year in which the genre seemed to make its presence felt with the most immediacy.

In Cold Blood, Truman Capote's "true account of a multiple murder and its consequences," appeared to a storm of controversy that year. Capote called the work a nonfiction novel and said that he had trained himself to remember what people said verbatim, therefore eliminating the necessity of taking notes as he interviewed people for his story. He said that his work was a "serious new art form," employing the reporter's research and the fiction writer's art. Capote used letters, diaries, interviews, and first-hand descriptions, along with carefully structured symbols, flashbacks, scenic telling, dialogue, and other techniques of the fiction writer. But Capote's factual accuracy was questioned by some critics, and although the book generated hundreds of imitators in the true-crime genre in the years following its publication, it also forced a debate about the nature of nonfiction and the ethical limits it cannot step beyond.

In Cold Blood was only a part of the more general literary debate during the 1960s, however. Tom Wolfe was acting as self-appointed spokesperson for the New Journalism, and John Barth took the lead in the popular press as the advocate for the new fabulists. Barth proclaimed that the realistic novel was dead, and Tom Wolfe said that the new journalists would gladly and constructively appropriate those techniques that the nineteenth-century novelists had left behind. Coover, Pynchon, Brautigan, Barthelme, and other novelists during that period were abandoning the techniques of realistic fiction because they felt that the contemporary world simply could not be represented by them. Novelists like Norman Mailer were trading allegiances somewhat and finding new possibilities in nonfiction with books such as *Armies of the Night* in 1968 and later *The Executioner's Song*. Journalists like Gay Talese found critical and popular success with nonfiction works such as *The Kingdom and the Power*, a book that employed his talents as a literary journalist to study the respected citadel of American journalism, the *New York Times*; and *Honor Thy Father*, which offered an inside look at the Mafia. Tom Wolfe attempted to sum up the decade in works like *The Electric Kool-Aid Acid Test, The Pump House Gang*, and *The Kandy-Kolored Tangerine-Flake Streamline Baby*. Michael Herr gave a surrealistic nonfiction account of the Vietnam War in *Dispatches*, published in 1977, and Joan Didion depicted the war on the home front in *Slouching Toward Bethlehem*. *Harper's, Atlantic Monthly*, and the *New Yorker* published a generation of literary journalists during the 1960s and 1970s. In March 1968 *Harper's* published Norman Mailer's "The Steps of the Pentagon," outdoing "Hiroshima" as the longest magazine article ever published— and perhaps equally controversial. Magazines like *Harper's*, as Willie Morris has said, reflected the time period and the writers used factual stories to "interpret it, shape it, criticize or goad it."[24]

McPhee and the New Journalism

The journalists who wrote for such magazines during those mercurial times helped shape the direction of literary nonfiction and gave rise to an entire generation of new writers—Tobias Wolff, Annie Dillard, Gretel Ehrlich, William Least Heat-Moon, Mark Singer, Richard Preston, and many others—as eclectic as any group of talented recent novelists. Few nonfiction writers, however, have demonstrated John McPhee's dazzling versatility and uncanny consistency. Since 1965, with the publication of *A Sense of Where You Are,* he has written twenty-three works of nonfiction to critical acclaim and popular attention. *A Sense of Where You Are* did not arrive on the literary scene with the same fanfare that *In Cold Blood* did, but it received good reviews and an appreciation that went beyond the ranks of basketball fans. Rex Lardner, in the *New York Times Book Review,* said that the book was "immensely well-written, inspiring without being preachy."[25] McPhee is highly respected by scholars and his fellow writers for his unyielding integrity in how he approaches writing about his subjects. He is admired by a following of readers for his ability to weave a narrative from what at times may appear to be the homeliest of fabrics. As William Howarth has pointed out, McPhee has a passion for details and a reverence for facts, but he also "packs an impressive bag of narrative tricks."[26] He has what Howarth aptly describes as a "ventriloquist's skill."

McPhee prefers not to be called a new journalist but rather sees himself an "old journalist" (Personal Interview). It is not difficult to see him as a scion of Joseph Mitchell and Henry David Thoreau, a craftsman, a writer, a reporter, an artist. Clearly, he is not a new journalist in the manner of a Hunter Thompson or Tom Wolfe. McPhee rarely announces his presence in his stories in any obvious way. Readers will not even find his photograph on his book jackets. He is pleasant and engaging in interviews but grants them only rarely. He does not follow the talk-show circuit when a new book of his is published. He believes that "an author can get between the reader and the work. A piece of writing is something in which the figure of the author is just one component. When I see this figure of an author on television, for instance, coming between the reader and the work, I think the reader loses something. The reader is the most creative thing in a piece of work. The writer puts down the words and the reader creates a scene. Writing is literally in the eye of the beholder. Therefore, the writer who is embedded in the text can distract the reader by coming forward. Creative reading is the issue. The reader is braiding many things together, and in that process the voice that comes through is important. In that sense, the reader creates the author" (Personal Interview). Instead of announcing his persona in his work, McPhee participates in the events he is dramatizing quietly, a gentle presence, a comic or mildly ironic voice. We do not see his face but we view the world through his eyes. As Joan Hamilton interprets his accomplishment, "His reputation is built around what Howarth calls 'scrupulous nonfiction,' fair-minded, meticulously researched products that illuminate a topic from all sides while keeping the author and his opinions in the shadows. McPhee's prose is also artful, full of well-rounded characters and well-told stories. He's a literary journalist, not a fact merchant."[27]

Critical opinion of McPhee's literary journalism over the past thirty years has been, essentially, uniformly flattering. Scholars like Kathy Smith conclude that "McPhee may well be regarded as a master tactician when it comes to maintaining both the integrity of the journalism profession and the art of writing."[28] And fellow writers like David Remnick, a new star at the *New Yorker,* feel "McPhee's work has the quality of permanence. Like Wilson's *Apologies to the Iroquois,* Mitchell's *McSorley's Wonderful Saloon,* Mark Singer's *Mr. Personality,* or Ian Frazier's *Great Plains,* McPhee's books represent the best of what has been in the *New Yorker* and are among the innovations in nonfiction writing."[29] Most critics and readers of his work have long been aware that McPhee's writing is much more than ordinary journalism. Robert Coles, writing in the *Washington Post* about *Coming into the Country,* said "Those human creatures McPhee stalks . . . have their own ironic grandeur. To face down a demanding, consuming external world is to be on to something psychologically, spiritually—existence converging toward essence. By showing us what Alaska is like, McPhee reminds us what we have become."[30]

McPhee's journalism goes deep into the heart of what it is to be American in the modern world, what it is to be human. He strikes a profound chord, but he does it subtly, not by philosophizing but by artfully telling the stories that he has brought back from Alaska or Florida or the New Jersey Pine Barrens. Creatively, he tells his story, arranging the facts along the narrative like beads on a necklace. His reputation is high, but as David Remnick argues, it "should be higher still." He is a writer of enormous gifts who has created a body of literary nonfiction that will last. And there is no sign that his powers are diminishing. As Remnick says, "Over the years, McPhee's writing, on all subjects, has evolved. The characters and narrative structures in his recent work are more complicated and surprising. He is looser, funnier, and at the same time his engagement with the physical world and moral problems has consistently deepened."[31] Ronald Weber also strikes to the center of McPhee's genius when he says, "It is not finally the use of certain techniques that makes nonfiction literary or journalism art, but the capacity to make factual experience meaningful through the process—as Bellow said—of giving weight and significance to the particular with resonant meanings."[32] For the past thirty years McPhee has demonstrated how reporting can be an art, how nonfiction can be literature, how facts can be used in the service of a higher truth.

Chapter Three

The Reporter as Artist

A Pastoral Vision

In 1946, at the age of fifteen, John McPhee sat with a friend on a windowsill of the Joseph Henry House, near the heart of the Princeton University campus. His friend's father was the Dean of the College and his friend's family lived there. Along with a few thousand other people, they listened to Harry S. Truman address a group of students on the occasion of the two hundreth anniversary of the university. People milled about, and attentive observers peered from other windows. When McPhee told me this story recently, as we stood near that very spot, he looked up at the window sill where he had sat nearly a half century ago and said, "It's a different country now. That building would be filled with Secret Service Men" (Personal Interview). McPhee is not generally prone to making political pronouncements in conversation or in his writing. He is not known as a polemist or a philosopher. He does not write about the crime-filled inner cities or the urban ills in America; however, his view of the world comes across dramatically, if implicitly, in his books, as it does, it seems to me, in this anecdote. His vision of the world is not sentimental, but it is pastoral. As James N. Stull explains in *Literary Selves: Autobiography and Contemporary American Nonfiction,* McPhee's "preoccupation with an older and more traditional America and its exemplary or model citizens suggests an idealized (pastoral), if not utopian, conception of the world."[1]

McPhee's America, delineated in nearly two dozen books, has its roots in the bucolic soil of Princeton and the idyllic shoreline of Keewaydin Camp. His America is populated with strong individualists; careful artisans; and unrecognized adventurers, do-ers, builders, and makers. McPhee, in this respect, is in the American grain, in the tradition of Benjamin Franklin, Ralph Waldo Emerson, and Henry David Thoreau. In his work he affirms, as Barbara Lounsberry suggests, the nineteenth-century values of self-reliance and individualism.[2] Like Thoreau, McPhee seems to cherish both the intellectual and the experiential, both the meditative and the active life. He reveals himself in the subjects he chooses to write about, in the characters he finds to admire.

In a typically dark comic manner, Mark Twain once reputedly defined life as the process in which one has a good time for the first third and spends the rest of the time recalling it. This is not exactly true of McPhee, who is the archetypal peripatetic journalist, traveling about in canoes, on merchant vessels, or through the bear-filled woods of northern Alaska, but it may be an appropriate comment on the influences that shaped McPhee's choices as far as the world he would choose to describe. The scientists, athletes, and outdoorsmen that he was surrounded by in Princeton and at Keewaydin shaped his vision of the world he would choose to represent to his readers. His choice of subject matter implicitly establishes his world view. As James Stull comments, "McPhee's construction of a stable, authentic, and old-fashioned American self is at once a retreat into certain pasts and a reaction to a social order increasingly characterized by fragmentation, the erosion of traditional values and beliefs, and the diminution of what was once called the imperial self."[3] McPhee offers a range of nonfiction that depicts the real world and an idealized world at the same time, but this does not mean that he is "some sort of Platonic version of a Yankee magazine staff writer."[4] Rather, as David Remnick points out, McPhee's work has a political edge to it implicitly but also explicitly: "McPhee is drawn to craftsmen, it is true, to experts who open up a world for him and his readers, but these voices invariably point their way toward questions large and, not infrequently, political. It soon becomes clear (or should) that amid all of McPhee's pursuit of personal pleasures in his choice of subjects (canoes, the wilderness, food, sport), he has been steadily, subtly developing a political literature.

Over time McPhee has become the "most effective literary advocate for environmentalism."[5] But even when he writes about the environment in a political context, as he does in *Encounters with the Archdruid, Coming into the Country,* and at times, *The Pine Barrens,* he offers no simple solutions to problems and appears to take no sides. He is a storyteller, and he allows the story to make its own point and for the reader to derive the philosophical or political lesson that might be there to be discovered. His principal goal as a writer, similar to most novelists, is to represent the lives of his individual characters. Most often it is the stories of people that he tells. Even in his rather technical quartet on geology, the figures that stand out are the central characters in each volume—Anita Harris, David Love, Eldridge Moores, or Kenneth Deffeyes—his guides into the mysteries of the earth. The overarching theme that connects all of his books, not just the geology works, may be the earth itself. The question he asks in *Coming into the Country*—"What will be the fate of this land?"—could well serve as an epigraph for the majority of his work. The question implies others—What will be the fate of those who inhabit the land? How do we preserve what is beautiful and distinct in the land and in humanity, as well? Can the spirit survive in a homogenized landscape of state parks and townhouses? Hardly ever does McPhee make such questions explicit in his stories. But his narratives, by their very nature, focus the reader's attention on his true subject—exemplary individuals, men and women who are independent and resourceful. Some are wayfarers, some are grounded in one place, a few are successful or famous, most are ordinary people doing unspectacular jobs, but all have a devotion to something in their lives and that gives them a form of sovereignty that seems rare in the contemporary world. Boyden has "the gift of authority," Bradley has "a sense of where you are," and farmers like Rich Hodgson know how "to give good weight." Many of McPhee's characters, like Bill Bradley, have a sense of their place in the world.

Immersion Reporting and Novelistic Techniques

Some critics have faulted McPhee for "over-admiring" his subjects or for not being enough of a "risk-taker," but it might be wise to remember Henry James's admonition about giving writers their *donnee*—that is, the reader should accept the premise of a writer's work and make a judgment about how well the work succeeds. McPhee communicates his vision of the world in the manner a novelist would—dramatically. To write a factual account with the dramatic techniques of a novelist, McPhee, like other literary journalists, must rely on immersion reporting. He must spend long hours interviewing a subject and watching a person work. He must give months to doing research in the library. He has to spend enough time with an interviewee to create a rapport, has to be there, notebook in hand, long enough for the person to say things he would not say even to his wife, as one of McPhee's profile subjects expressed it.

To write *Coming into the Country*, McPhee spent months at a time over a two-year period in different parts of Alaska. To write *The Pine Barrens*, he made numerous journeys during the course of a year into the wilderness section of New Jersey, spending time with Fred Brown and others. To write "Travels in Georgia," he drove over 1,000 miles of southern back roads, examining roadkill and taking inventory of wild places left in the state with field zoologist Carol Ruckdeschel. Immersion reporters have to do their research, but they also have to attend patiently to their subjects. Mark Kramer explains it this way: "You have to stay around a long time before people will let you get to know them. They're guarded the first time and the second time and the first ten times. Then you get boring. They forget you're there. Or else they've had a chance to make you into something in their world. They make you into a surgical resident or they make you into a farmhand or a member of the family. And you let it happen."[6]

Most of the people McPhee writes about he has never met before. There have been a couple he knew beforehand—Alan Lieb in "Brigade de Cuisine," Thomas Hoving in "A Roomful of Hovings," and Frank L. Boyden in *The Headmaster*—but the vast majority of his stories have been about people he seeks out for the purpose of writing about them. In the process, he becomes friends with some—Bill Bradley, Sam Candler, or Captain Paul Washburn—but with all he must develop a sense of trust. David Brower, whom McPhee wrote about in *Encounters with the Archdruid,* said that the entire Brower family responded to the writer's presence the year that he was working on his interviews with the environmentalist. "He was casting director, amusing and assiduous," Brower said. "We all fell in love with him."[7]

McPhee has said that "you've got to understand a lot to write even a little bit."[8] And research in the library and a brief interview with a subject simply will not give the writer of literary nonfiction the requisite information. The writer needs to be *there,* with the subject in her job on the back roads of Georgia or on his merchant ship, scribbling, always scribbling in a notebook. The information that such immersion reporting will give the writer is the source of many of the novelistic techniques that will be available to him, techniques such as point of view, description, scenic telling, symbolism, voice. McPhee uses all of these techniques in his various books with great skill and integrity. In *The Pine Barrens,* for example, he offers a scene that tells the reader with novelistic grace a great deal about the two Pineys McPhee has encountered in his search for a drink of water:

> Fred said, "They could build ten jetports around me. I wouldn't give a damn."
>
> "You ain't going to be around very long," Bill said to him. "It would be the end of these woods."
>
> Fred took that as a fact, and not an insult. "Yes, it would be the end of these woods," he said. "But there'd be people here you could do business with."

Bill said, "There ain't no place like this left in the country, I don't believe—and I traveled around a little bit, too." Eventually, I made the request I had intended to make when I walked in the door. "Could I have some water?" I said to Fred. "I have a jerry can and I'd like to fill it at the pump."

"Hell, yes," he said. "That isn't my water. That's God's water. That's God's water. That right, Bill?"

"I guess so," Bill said, without looking up. "It's good water, I can tell you that."

"That's God's water," Fred said again. "Take all you want." (*Pine*, 13)

In this scene, McPhee gives subtle clues to Fred's character and Bill's, as well. He introduces the significance of the water, which runs like a symbolic stream throughout the narrative. He sets the stage for an exploration of the area, "a separate world," and its people, shy, self-sufficient, and much-maligned.

In *Levels of the Game,* his depiction of a U.S. Open semifinal match between Arthur Ashe and Clark Graebner, early in the story he draws the reader into a novelistic point of view:

Ashe has crossed no man's land and is already astride the line between the service boxes, waiting to volley. Only an extraordinarily fast human being could make a move of that distance so quickly. Graebner's return is a good one. It comes low over the net and descends toward Ashe's backhand. Ashe will not be able to hit the ball with power from down there. Having no choice, he hits it up, and weakly—but deep—to Graebner's backhand.

Graebner is mindful of his strategy: Just hit the ball in the court, Clark. Just hit the ball in the court. . . . Surely this particular shot is a setup, a sitter, hanging there soft and helpless in the air. With a vicious backhand drive, Graebner tries to blow the ball cross court, past Ashe. But it goes into the net. Fifteen-love. (*Levels,* 4–5)

There is a thrilling tension in this scene, an intimation of Graebner's character, an intimation that will grow into a well-rounded characterization by the end of the story. There is also the unusual point of view for the nonfiction story. McPhee, the nonfiction writer, gets inside the heads of his main characters. Like readers of fiction, we watch the scene and listen to the characters' thoughts, as well. McPhee was able to use this technique because he viewed film of the match with both Ashe and Graebner and was able to record their memories of what they were thinking at crucial moments in the match.

Structure and the Limits of Nonfiction

The voice in McPhee's books is clear and laced with graceful good humor. There is ample evidence of his gentle wit in his stories—odd facts, unusual metaphors, self-deprecatory digressions—but his writing style acts like a window to the world, not a mirror to his own personality. Sandra Schmidt Oddo, in the *New York Times Book Review* in 1974, summed up McPhee's style with precision: "McPhee's style is Journalism 101 elevated to the ranks of Art. He uses short sentences, no passive verbs, paragraphs that pursue their subjects with flat-statement, single-minded intensity. He uses them—the art of it—with easy grace, fluidity; and he has the courage to drop raw observations into seemingly unrelated contexts and leave them there reverberating as signals for the reader to interpret. He is also very, very good at breaking down specialized jargon into plain English, at interpreting the ways of scientists for the layman, at understanding and enjoying processes of thought, of invention, of human behavior."[9]

Whatever novelistic techniques that McPhee uses—symbolism, scenic telling, internal point of view—he always keeps his work grounded in a clear style and a sense of the verifiable facts. Not all scholars, however, feel that it is possible for any writer to stay anchored truly in the facts. Kathy Smith, in her article "John McPhee Balances the Act," argues, it seems, for the mutability of all facts and the impossibility of writing without creating a fiction. "But despite McPhee's insistence on the power of truth, the way in which representation occurs always depends on artifice. The author disguises himself as recorder in order to temper the mediation between fact and story and to promote the 'real illusion' that structure itself provides a natural and absolute system of identification rather than a true replica that is produced in the midst of narrative adventure."[10] But McPhee responds to this talk of a "fictionalizing act" with an unaccustomed tartness: "That's just academic air. Of course, there's definite truth in it, the idea that all writing is fiction. I agree with the idea if you express it in a certain way. You can't exactly reproduce human life; everything is a little bit of illusion. So what? Ho, hum. Everyone knows that at the start. The important gradation in the whole thing is that you get as close as you can to what you saw and heard" (Personal Interview). For McPhee, although he acknowledges that all writing is a construct, it is absolutely essential that the nonfiction writer does not invent words or actions for his characters. The writer can use the tools of invention, such as point of view and dialogue, but the writer must not invent the facts. The writer should not allow his vision of things to change the subject, but rather the information that the writer gathers should force him to reshape his view of the particular world he is writing about.

Nonfiction writers have an implicit but binding contract with their readers. One bit of fakery diminishes the credibility of the whole enterprise. As McPhee once said, "Nonfiction writing is like an aquifer: one pollutant can spread through it and taint it all." (Personal Interview)

Many readers agree with W. Ross Winterowd that "McPhee's genius is his ability to use a narrative structure as a vehicle for conveying facts and judgments, a rhetorical technique characteristic of good journalism."[11] McPhee is renowned for his mastery of structure, for the inventiveness of his individual profiles of a Bill Bradley or Frank Boyden, the intricacy of the contrapuntal movement of a dual profile such as *Levels of the Game,* or the triadic structure of an intricate book like *Encounters with the Archdruid.* In an important respect, a large part of McPhee's artistry is to be found in his structuring of his material.

It may be no coincidence that one of McPhee's daughters is a professor of architectural history. An interest in architecture may be in the genes, for each of McPhee's books has a well-designed architectural plan. For McPhee, structure is as much a creative tool as metaphor or point of view. He tries to stay open to the various possibilities for structure that a given piece of writing might offer. "Each piece of writing has a structure embedded in it," he once said (Personal Interview). Most often, McPhee seems to seek an organic structure, a pattern that is true to the central themes the story dramatizes. Given his concern for the earth, it comes as no surprise that many of his books are concerned with circles. In a phone interview with Barbara Lounsberry, he said, "Everything I write about is round."[12] And it seems true—there are basketballs, bombs, cranberries, atoms, tennis balls, oranges, dirigible-like aircraft, spheres, concentric circles, the earth itself. In *Coming into the Country,* for instance, McPhee compares the beauty of "the great land" to a uniqueness "composed in turning circles," and one critic astutely pointed out that the three sections of the book dramatize "interlocking circles, each with its representative Alaskan emblem."[13] The first section of the book, entitled "The Encircled River," recounts a canoe and kayak trip that McPhee took with four companions down the pristine Salmon and Kobuk Rivers in the virtually uninhabited Brooks range in northern Alaska. The story begins with these sentences: "My bandanna is rolled on the diagonal and retains water fairly well. I keep it knotted around my head, and now and again dip it into the river" (*Country*, 5). And it ends with the image of the dry bandanna (*Country*, 95). The story begins with the circle of the bandanna and the circular journey that these men are on. McPhee looks down into the river at the salmon swimming there and to him it looks like a "sky full of zeppelins." He sees a male salmon "circling" a female, "an endless attention of rings." At the conclusion of the chapter, although McPhee and his companions have not fully circled their territory, the circle is complete, the sense of the natural cycles that make up Alaska is clear. But even if the circle of the sun has once again appeared, "spraying up the light," the final circle has dark possibilities, as the canoeists drift past a mutilated salmon.

Not all of McPhee's books develop from what appears to be an organic structure. Some, like *Levels of the Game* or *Encounters with the Archdruid,* are more clearly superimposed structures that McPhee invents for the purpose of the story. These structures have a subtlety and logic to them. In a sense, structure is always an invention of the writer, whether we call the structure internal or external, organic or artificial. The difference may be a matter of direction. In creating an organic structure, the writer derives a pattern in the materials and uses that pattern to hold the narrative together. In a superimposed structure, the writer first decides on a pattern that will hold the given story together and collects or sifts the material accordingly. In *Encounters with the Archdruid,* for example, McPhee claims that it was the very challenge of structure that led him to write about the environmental visionary David Brower. McPhee decided that he wanted to try a triadic sort of profile, an "A-B-C over D" configuration for a narrative. After he determined to attempt such a structure, he then looked for a fitting subject. All sorts of ideas floated by—an architect and three clients, a choreographer and three dancers, a director and three actors. A deep interest in the natural world led him to write about Brower, the Archdruid of the environmental movement, and three pro-development people. In *Levels of the Game,* McPhee's desire to go beyond the single-person profile led him to the tennis match between Ashe and Graebner and led him to the film sessions that would allow him a logical contrapuntal structure, a serve and volley approach that mirrored the game itself.

At times, necessity is the catalyst for invention as far as structure is concerned. McPhee had a difficult time writing *The Survival of the Bark Canoe,* his portrait of the craftsman Henri Vaillancourt. As McPhee has said, it should have been an easy story for him to write. It was a story about a canoe builder by a man who had spent most of his life riding

around in canoes, but Vaillancourt turned out not to be the character
that McPhee expected:

> That latter part [of *The Survival of the Bark Canoe*] had a profound
> influence on the structure of the story. He was what an English professor
> might call an unsympathetic character. I developed a structure different
> from the one I would have chosen had he been more sympathetic. If I
> hadn't had any special problems with that piece of writing, I probably
> would have begun it with the canoe trip or in the trip. I mean, look at
> the other pieces of mine that involve journeys. They begin in the middle,
> they flash back. . . . If I'd done this story the same way, I would have
> started somewhere on the trip. . . . So why are these seven thousand
> words first? Because a reader goes through a process of learning about a
> character, and I wanted the reader to appreciate Henri's skills without
> being prejudiced by a description of his behavior on the canoe trip.[14]

Like any creative writer, McPhee imposes order on his materials to
arrive at a truth. Materials must be fashioned and shaped. Whether the
structure is organic or mechanical, whether the pattern of the story follows the life cycle of the orange or a prescribed trip along fault lines, the
writer must find a structure that works without calling attention to
itself. Structure is there to advance characterization or to help communicate theme; it is an aesthetic tool, not an end in itself. "Readers are not
supposed to be aware of structure," McPhee says, "but its logic may
bring them into the story" (Personal Interview).

Writing Methods

McPhee's writing methodology was first discussed, and perhaps still
definitively so, by William Howarth in his Introduction to *The John
McPhee Reader*.[15] Howarth describes a man whose preparatory outlines
would have made Olive McKee beam with pride. After McPhee has
decided on a topic, travel usually takes up a great deal of his time in the
early stages of the writing process. He could be in Switzerland, studying
the inner workings of the Swiss Army, or in Nevada, investigating mod-
ern-day cattle rustling. He tries to go out with only the most rudimen-
tary knowledge of the subject, enough preparation so that he is not
wasting the subject's time, and as few preconceptions as possible. He
does not go out with a prepared set of questions or a fixed notion of

what should happen. He carries a stack of four-by-six-inch spiral note-books with him, and in his left-handed script he scribbles furiously his own brand of shorthand. He describes this part of his writing this way: "I put down anything that I want to remember, including sketches of people, what they're wearing, what they're saying, how they look, whether they're sunburned—whatever it is, I want to remember it. The notebooks contain a great deal more than answers to the questions I ask."[16] When he gets home to Princeton, he types up his notes. The notes expand somewhat as he adds ideas about possible structures or potential asides. More research may occur at this point and more addi-tions. Before McPhee had a computer, he used to cut up a copy of his notes with a pair of scissors and sort the pieces into different folders. He then would code the folders with structural topics and assemble them on index cards. With the index cards he would play what William Howarth termed "a sort of writer's solitaire," examining the different ways of organizing the material. After he determined the right order for the cards he would tack them to a bulletin board and code a duplicate set of typed notes, cutting sentences and paragraphs into thousands of scraps that he would sort into a new set of file folders to match the newly discovered structure. Now, the computer program created for him by Howard Strauss at Princeton University allows him to sort and categorize blocks of information. As McPhee once said to me, "These computer programs permit me to do the same thing I did in the tenth century, when I started writing. One of the programs implodes informa-tion, the other explodes it" (Personal Interview). The computer program allows him to work more efficiently and minus some of the clutter. He still does the note cards, though, moving them around the office until he finds the right order.

After organizing the material, McPhee writes the first draft. He prints it out, about nineteen lines to the page so that he has plenty of space for additions, deletions, changes, and edits with a pencil. In an interview McPhee said, "Very often I write so much on that page that the original is almost obscured. That's the way I go through the whole second draft. For *Assembling California,* that process took six months with the computer off except at the end of each day, when I'd put in what I'd done."[17]

As Howarth says, this kind of description of McPhee's writing methodology makes the whole enterprise seem mechanical, almost too controlled, but for McPhee it is that very sort of preparation that gives him the room to be creative, to find the precarious balances among characters and facts, to discover interesting metaphors, to craft a telling scene. It is this sort of preparation that helps him to fashion journalism with the resonances of literature. With an habitual modesty, John McPhee refers to himself as a reporter, but if he retains some of the methods of a good journalist, his finished work proves that he is an artist.

Chapter Four

The McPhee Hero

The *New Yorker* Profile

In a sense, all of John McPhee's books are profiles, the stories of individual lives, for as he says, "I write about real people in real places. All of my work is about that" (Personal Interview). His profiles are in the tradition of the *New Yorker* profiles, a form that was supposedly named by that magazine's first Talk of the Town writer and editor, James McGuinness. Harold Ross, the magazine's founder and first editor, wanted stories in which subjects were sketched in quick outline. In the early years of the magazine that is exactly what the profiles were, slight sketches, but within a few years writers like A. J. Liebling, St. Clair McKelway, and Joseph Mitchell were making these stories, as Thomas Kunkel phrased it, "more muscular and multifaceted" than they had been before.[1] Profiles from the *New Yorker* became renowned for their intricacy and clarity, their attention to detail, and their variety. In the mid-1960s the magazine provided the richest ground possible for McPhee's style of writing to flourish. As he has said, "Things have always been allowed to grow there and reach their own natural length, whatever that might be. They were not written to fit a certain space. A piece of writing is a piece of writing, whether it's a haiku or the Anglo-Saxon Chronicle, and when I started at the magazine I never had the onerous sense that my stories had to fit any kind of mold. They had to be as long as they had to be and not one smidgen more" (Personal Interview).

The *New Yorker* gave its writers the encouragement of a high standard for its profiles and the relaxed deadlines to shape the narrative in the necessary ways. For staff writers, like McPhee, that meant the freedom to explore the possibilities in a story. In a eulogistic essay in the 28 December 1992 issue of the *New Yorker,* in writing about his relationship with the editor William Shawn, McPhee sheds quite a bit of light on what the magazine offered him as a young writer of profiles:

> He [Shawn] understood the disjunct kinship of creative work—every
> kind of creative work—and time. The most concise summation of it I've

ever heard was seven words he said just before closing my first Profile and sending it off to press. It was 1965, and I was a new young writer, and he did not entrust new writers to any extent whatever to other editors. He got the new ones started by himself. So there we were—hours at a session—discussing reverse pivots and backdoor plays and the role of the left-handed comma in the architectonics of basketball while the *New Yorker* hurtled toward its deadlines. I finally had to ask him, "How can you afford to use so much time and go into so many things in such detail when the whole enterprise is yours to keep together?"

He said, "It takes as long as it takes."

As a part-time writing teacher, I have offered those words to a generation of students. If they are serious writers, they will never forget them.[2]

A Sense of Where You Are

McPhee began writing profiles during his years at *Time* magazine, but his breakthrough with the *New Yorker* came with his story about Bill Bradley, *A Sense of Where You Are*. As he told Norman Sims, "It was the Bradley piece that changed my life."[3] *A Sense of Where You Are*, which was published as a book after the article appeared in the magazine, is not McPhee's most intricate or complex profile, but it is, nevertheless, a striking piece of writing, detailed, dramatic, lucid, lyrical. It also offers the first view of the McPhee hero, what Barbara Lounsberry calls his Emersonian "representative man or woman."[4] In *A Sense of Where You Are*, Lounsberry says, McPhee's "artistic vision is most simply and purely revealed."[5] In a sense, although the book, like all of McPhee's narratives, appears to be strictly realistic, a perfect example of journalistic mimesis, it is actually a reflexive piece of work. *A Sense of Where You Are* reveals as much about the writer as it does about his subject.

A Sense of Where You Are, dedicated to McPhee's father, defines McPhee, the artist. On the surface, the story is about basketball, but the underlying text tells the tale of a craftsman or artist. The six-foot-five-inch Bradley is an Olympian image of McPhee himself. Both played basketball, both went to Princeton, both took a postgraduate year in England, but the profile does not weigh these similarities. Rather, it recounts Bradley's story, after mentioning some of the analogies. By implication, though, it connects the two men, their two stories, the athlete and the writer. Both are craftsmen. At one point in the narrative McPhee writes, "The metaphor of basketball is to be found in these compounding alternatives. Every time a basketball player takes a step, an entire new geometry of action is created around him. In ten seconds, with or without the ball, a good player may see perhaps a hundred alternatives, and, from them, make half a dozen choices as he goes along. A great player will see even more alternatives and will make more choices, and this multiradial way of looking at things can carry over into his life" (*Sense*, 49).

The metaphor of writing may also be found in the notion of compounding alternatives, and in many of his discussions of craft, McPhee has suggested that fact. Speaking to Norman Sims, McPhee said, "There are lots of ideas going by. A huge stream. What makes somebody choose one over another?"[6] The writer faces choices in subject matter; in characters, details, and themes; and in structures. In writing, as in basketball, one thing often leads to another; one choice shapes the next set of possibilities.

McPhee and Bradley are much alike in their search for structures that will serve well but inconspicuously. Describing Bradley's game, McPhee could as well be commenting on his own goals as a writer: "With all his analyses of its mechanics, Bradley may have broken down his game into its components, but he has reassembled it so seamlessly that all the parts, and also his thousand hours of practice, are concealed" (*Sense*, 81). For McPhee, Bradley is the "truly complete basketball player" (29), and everything that he does on the court he does "with a floating economy of motion and a beguiling offhandedness that appeal to the imagination" (81). For both men, the proper mechanics are crucial, but if they show, then they are clumsy. McPhee's description of Bradley's performance on the court is, in essence, a description of much of what he values in good writing, or in any activity, for that matter. With Bradley, "Every motion developed in its simplest form. Every motion repeated itself precisely when he used it again" (5). Bradley does not like "flamboyance," and unlike contemporary players, he "apparently never made a move merely to attract attention" (20–1).

As *A Sense of Where You Are* makes clear, basketball players, like writers perhaps, need "to be able to see a little more than the next man" (*Sense*, 62). And for the great player, like Bradley, that means having a special vision, "a sense of where you are." This special vision, this intuition, may be a gift, but McPhee makes a point of recounting the fact that Bradley spent a good deal of his time during his youth in Crystal City, Missouri, trying to expand his peripheral vision by walking down the street, his eyes focused straight ahead, while he attempted to pick out items in the windows of the stores that he was passing. McPhee, like Bradley, is detail oriented, and he offers several pieces of information that suggest the intimate relationship between Bradley and his environment, the basketball court. In one instance, McPhee describes Bradley's practicing at the Lawrenceville School, shooting jump shots, missing one after another until he adjusted to the new basket. After hitting four shots in a row, Bradley said to McPhee, "You want to know something? That basket is about an inch and a half low" (28). A few weeks later, McPhee, the reporter, went back to the gym with a measuring tape and a ladder. The rim was exactly one and one-eighths inches too low. Both writer and player have a sense of where they are in their own mediums.

Bradley is an artist-hero, a man who performs with great skill and humility, a democratic ideal, caring more for the group than he does for himself, an individual with the ability to act and the intellect to understand and explain his actions. Bradley also has a sense of perspective. He strives to be an accomplished scholar, a good citizen, a positive influence on his teammates. He is named by his classmates as the best athlete, "as a kind of afterthought" (144). As David Remnick points out, McPhee discovered in Bradley "a perfect subject, one who could articulate his own distinctive character, verbally and physically." In the same article, Remnick goes on to say that "In Bradley, McPhee found an artist in absolute touch with his materials (his teammates, the court, his own body) and willing to describe them."[7]

Bradley, then, is the first of the McPhee heroes—dedicated to his craft, meticulous, articulate, engaged deeply in the world around him, defining himself and, to a certain extent, the world by his vocation. McPhee's heroes are men and women who are "called" to the world by their vocations. McPhee has been accused of being too easy on some of the subjects of his profiles, and David Remnick even describes one of McPhee's portraits (in a positive light) as "hagiography."[8] Remnick has struck on exactly the right word, I believe, for from the start McPhee has chosen subjects for his profiles that are close to his heart, close to his own interests, and emblematic of his own vision of the world. Therefore, it is logical that he writes what seem at times to be saints' legends, tales of representative men and women, idealized but real Americans.

Bradley is the epitome of the basketball player. In the consolation game, against Wichita State, his team wins 118 to 82, going farther than any Princeton team ever did in the NCAA championships. All sorts of other records fell to the young hero, as well, but when he returns to his campus, he apologizes to the crowd for letting them down, for losing to Michigan. Not even his fifty-eight points and record-breaking performance skew his vision and distort his sense of importance in the world. As Barbara Lounsberry explains, "Bradley is the representative man, one who represents not only the highest levels of achievement in his field, but unites the field within himself. Here is the link of the whole, the representative figure, the one, with the many. . . . McPhee's representative men, like Emerson's, exert spiritual as well as physical or intellectual leadership. 'The world is upheld by the veracity of good men,' wrote Emerson in *Representative Men;* 'they make the earth wholesome.' "[9] Thus, it is reasonable for David Remnick to refer to *A Sense of Where You Are* as "sports hagiography," for this is not a portrait that reflects the average and flawed individual but rather the best we can hope to become.

The Headmaster

In *The Headmaster,* McPhee's profile of Frank L. Boyden, who was the head of Deerfield Academy when McPhee attended the school from 1948 to 1949, he continues in the pattern that he began in *A Sense of Where You Are.* This time he focuses his attention on "an educator by intuition" (*Headmaster,* 7). Like Bradley, Boyden is a representative man, "in all probability, the last man of his kind" (7). Similar to Bradley, the perfectionist who practices just one more shot, always one more shot, drawing his teammates up to their best performance, Boyden employs his unflagging energy, his humanity, and his scrupulous awareness of everything that is going on around him to educate the boys at the school. Boyden, too, has a precise sense of his surroundings, a sense of where he is, a clear idea of his place in the world. The headmaster at Deerfield for sixty-four years when McPhee wrote the book, Boyden is "a simple man with the gift of authority" (14), who has "spent his life building a school according to elemental ideas, but only a complicated man could bring off what he has done, and on the practical plane, he is full of paradox and politics" (13). Deviating slightly from his methodology in *A Sense of Where You Are,* McPhee offers some apparently striking contrasting images of Boyden from those who know him well—ruthless or a great humanitarian, thoughtful or thoughtless, stubborn or discerning, benevolent or feudal (14). Even one of his own sons says that Boyden views himself as "indestructible and infallible" (13).

   In the final analysis, however, *The Headmaster* is also the depiction of a representative man, an ideal. Boyden is an educator who has practiced his craft for more than a half century, and he is an artist, of sorts, doing his job by intuition, always having a sense of his place in his world.

Rules and regulations are not the essence of things for Boyden. Quoting
Robert E. Lee, he says, "A boy is more important than any rule" (19).
Boyden is a benevolent despot, but the emphasis falls on his benevo-
lence. His humanity and his educational insights are instinctive, it
seems:

> He seemed to know when there was something in a boy when on the
> surface there appeared to be nothing. He could assess this potentiality in
> a way that no test could, and he had the talent to help the boy reach it.
> In the nineteen-twenties, Deerfield regularly had a number of students
> who, for disciplinary or academic reasons, had been kicked out of places
> like Andover, Exeter, and Taft. After a year or two at Deerfield, a consid-
> erable number of these boys out-performed their former Exeter,
> Andover, or Taft classmates in college. This was not only gratifying to
> Boyden but pleasing and relieving to other headmasters, who suddenly
> found that with clear consciences they could fire almost any boy, since
> Frank Boyden could be counted on to turn the lout into an interested
> scholar and a useful citizen. (54)

There is not much criticism in this character study, and when criticism appears it is muted by a comic tone—"At Deerfield, all ranks
between five-star general and the noncommissioned officer are vacant"
(64). McPhee sketches Boyden's idiosyncratic character—his three-
minute naps before meetings with parents, his full-throttle uninhibited
driving of his golf cart around the campus, his wily political maneu-
vers—but the portrait, as Norman Sims says, is "polished but not critical." As Sims interprets the work, the story could not offer criticism
"because it lacked a character who would voice any criticisms. In Boyden, McPhee found a person similar to Bill Bradley. Boyden was a
strong personality who had a firm, 'straight arrow' moral code, was perhaps the best in the country at what he did, and was a local hero who
operated on a national level. Boyden left his mark on the boys in the
form of ethical standards, not academics."[10] Clearly, Boyden is a model
citizen, a man among men, fitting readily, perhaps, into what Kathy
Smith calls a "master narrative of heroism."[11] He is a symbolic figure as
much as he is a real one. The essayist Edward Hoagland, who attended
Deerfield around the same time that McPhee did, has said that
McPhee's profile of Boyden "records all the good things that might have
been said for [Boyden] and the school but few of the bad."[12] For his part,
McPhee has said that if he has any regrets about his work in its entirety,
"it's about one or two people I've lionized."[13] McPhee does not seem to

have those sorts of regrets about his portrait of Boyden (Personal Interview), and perhaps William Howarth may have come closest to summing up the achievement of the story when he wrote: "For all its sentiment, McPhee's profile of Boyden, like the man and his school, is 'drier than a covered bridge—solid, spare, and built to last, regardless of the traffic that passes through.' "[14]

Oranges

In his third book, *Oranges,* published in 1967, McPhee moved away from the traditional profile and offered, instead, an eclectic blend of history, process analysis, and character study. It is actually the story of the orange, in all its fascinating esoterica. But squeeze all of the botanical tidbits and the historical anecdotes from *Oranges* and there is still a core of profiles that give the story a human face. McPhee offers a brief but evocative description of orange pickers and in particular of Doyle Waid, a twenty-nine-year-old master of the trade. For McPhee, these pickers in general, like Steinbeck's migrant workers in *The Grapes of Wrath,* are an "admirable group," with a toughness and strength of spirit necessary for a difficult task. The best of them, like Doyle Waid, are experts reminiscent of Boyden and Bradley. In explaining his job to McPhee, Waid says, "That tree is good picking. . . . It's got big fruit. It's easy to ladder. You can set your ladder in there and get your inside fruit good. That's a bad tree next to it, with the branches close together. It's hard set. A good, average tree, it oughtn't to take over seven sets to get it" (*Oranges,* 57). A bit less polished in his speech than Bradley or Boyden, Waid nevertheless speaks knowledgeably and with enthusiasm about his job. His analysis of fruit picking does not sound all that different from Bradley's analysis of the five parts of a hook shot: " 'Crouch,' he says, crouching, and goes on to demonstrate the other moves. 'Turn your head to look for the basket, step, kick, follow through with your arms' " (*Sense,* 24).

Oranges stepped outside the traditional boundaries for the profile as far as subject matter and the lack of emphasis overall on characterizations were concerned. For this reason, there were some mixed reviews. The reviewer for *Harper's* thought it was a surprising accomplishment, "more absorbing than many a novel," but the reviewer for the *New York Times* thought the book unsuccessful, an unintentional parody of trivial *New Yorker* subject matter.[15] The reason that the book works for many readers, despite its unpromising subject matter, is because McPhee is able to skillfully mix history, character sketches, botany, and big business, and keep his sense of humor, as well. For instance, in describing contemporary orange auctions at Pier 28 at the western end of Canal Street in New York City, he says,

> The room seems to contain about ninety men and ninety lighted cigars. In London in the eighteenth century, oranges were auctioned "by the candle." A pin was pushed through a candle not far from the top, and when the candle was lighted, the bidding began. When the pin dropped, the most recent bidder got the oranges. In New York in the present era, oranges appear to be auctioned by cigar. The air in the auction room gets so heavy with smoke that if anything as light as a pin were to drop, it would probably stop falling before it reached the floor. (*Oranges,* 117)

A Roomful of Hovings

In 1968, the year after *Oranges* was published, McPhee came out with his first collection of shorter profiles from the *New Yorker, A Roomful of Hovings and Other Profiles*. In particular, in the titular story, "A Roomful of Hovings," the reader can see McPhee making more sophisticated use of the profile form than he had previously. The portrait of Thomas Hoving, then Director of the Metropolitan Museum of Art, is more complex structurally and psychologically than his characterizations of Bradley and Boyden. As McPhee envisioned Hoving's life, a number of themes ran through it. To paint the various pictures that he saw, McPhee had to decide upon a structural pattern that seemed fitting, a "gallery, a roomful of eleven portraits," as William Howarth defines it. Rather than tell the story chronologically, he told it thematically, creating a structure that he has compared to a capital "Y." As Norman Sims describes the structure of the work, "The descending branches finally joined at a moment of an epiphany during Hoving's college career at Princeton, and then proceeded along the bottom stem in a single line. McPhee maintained time sequences within each episode, but the themes were arranged to set up their dramatic juxtaposition."[16] This structure allows the reader to feel like a visitor to a museum, roaming from room to room, making judgments about various portraits, placing each aspect of Hoving's character in the context of the whole man. In the roomful of Hovings that McPhee creates, the reader is given a man of many nuances and talents, a personality with as many facets as a diamond, a man who "couldn't stand being categorized into one era." (*Roomful,* 64) McPhee draws pictures of the sternly ethical salesman, the wild teenager on Martha's Vineyard, the keen-eyed curatorial assistant at The Clois-

ters Museum in New York City, the indifferent schoolboy, the son of a
famous and successful father, the brilliant art historian.

The convergence of the two branches of the "Y" into the central line
of the story comes in the section titled "Princeton," which details Hovings' years as an undergraduate. Until his sophomore year at Princeton,
Hoving lived the life of a young Augustine, playing cards, drinking
Drambuie, vodka, and gin, and slipping off to the Orpheum Dance
Palace near Times Square in New York. But in the second term of his
sophomore year, he signed up for a course in sculpture from the Renaissance to the present, an experience that lifted his confidence and convinced him to major in art and archeology. From that moment on, the
sinner turned saint, and "he retreated from nearly all nonacademic
activity of any kind, roomed alone during his last two years, and was sel-
dom seen even by his friends" (50).

Once Hoving found his true passion, his real character, it seems,
emerged. Like Bradley, he is articulate, willing and able to analyze the
specifics of his vocation: "You peel a work of art like an onion. Shred
every layer from it. Is it in the style of the time? How many styles exist
within it? Study the iconography and the manner in which it is handled.
What does it intend to say? Parallels, parallels, always seek parallels.
Use scientific means—ultraviolet light, X-rays, and so forth—but
always in context with your eye. Scientific analyses can be used for or
against a work, like statistics. Your eye is king" (22–3). Although he
came a bit later to his calling than Bradley did, Hoving, too, has a sense
of his place in the world. "The only way to know art history," he says, "is
to be saturated. . . . You *know* what the forgers do" (23). Intuition,
peripheral vision, seeing—all of McPhee's "artists" have a sense of where
they are, which comes in part from their immersion in the activity that
they love.

"A Forager"

In the volume *A Roomful of Hoving and Other Profiles,* McPhee also portrays Euell Gibbons, nature writer and wild food expert, in "A Forager."
Gibbons' activities strike close to McPhee's interest in the wilderness
and in finding an ecological balance. But McPhee seems well aware of
Gibbons' reputation in some circles as a bit of an eccentric. "Gibbons'
interest in wild food suggests but does not actually approach madness.
He eats acorns because he likes them. He is neither ascetic or an
obsessed nutritionist" (*Roomful,* 69). It seems to be McPhee's purpose in

the story to discover who the true Gibbons is, the man behind the persona, and to do that he creates a journey that will structure his investigation. Early in the story, McPhee explains that, through letters and telephone calls, he framed a six-day foraging trip by canoe and on foot down the Susquehanna River and on the Appalachian Trail with Gibbons as forager-guide. It is a structure that granted McPhee enough time to see a pattern in Gibbons' life and career.

Gibbons, too, of course, is an expert who must rely on seeing, being able to recognize the benign mushrooms and avoid the poisonous ones. He is a man who can reach through the White House fence and harvest "four edible weeds from the President's garden" or collect some "satisfying snacks in concrete flower tubs in the mall at Rockefeller Center" (68). He recognizes what is around him even when most other people are unable to see the obvious. Gibbons is able to "read the land as if it were a language" (107).

McPhee does some foraging of his own into Gibbons' past, and along the way he shares some aspects of Gibbons' character that may have been hidden from most people's views of the man. In flashbacks along the way, McPhee tells of Gibbons' first marriage, his search for a career, his time as a bindle stiff, his beach combing in Hawaii. He recounts the poverty and hunger that Gibbons endured in his youth juxtaposed next to Gibbons' serio-comic foraging on their trip. Comedy and drama mix, as do past and present: Gibbons' mantra-like "you couldn't say we're suffering like the early Christians" or his amusing talk about pork chops or fried chicken as he collects wintergreen or watercress mix with his recounting having joined the Communist Party in his younger days or his becoming a Quaker. Gibbons is not the simple version that some people would have him be. He is, similar to McPhee, a man whose activity makes him difficult to define in simple terms. Gibbons' freezer contains not only wild foods, but Pepperidge Farm bread and Birds Eye lima beans, as well. When it comes to paying the county assessor's Occupation Tax and he tells the tax collector what he does for a living, the confused assessor lists him as a "part-time laborer" (114). McPhee knows better, though, for he sees that Gibbons is "the greatest living wild chef" (118).

"Brigade de Cuisine"

In 1978, about ten years after he published "A Forager," McPhee wrote about another chef-artist in "Brigade de Cuisine," which was reprinted

in *Giving Good Weight.* The story caused a small controversy as food critics turned detective to find out the name of the chef and the restaurant
about which McPhee wrote. McPhee had called the chef Otto (his real
name was Alan Lieb) and left the restaurant unidentified. The food
reviewers eventually found Otto in Shohola, Pennsylvania. In part, the
food critics were provoked by the thought that a great chef could be
operating a business close to New York City and they did not know
about him.

Like many of McPhee's subjects, Otto was not interested in celebrity
but in the work he performs. In watching him work, we see the essence
of the man. One of Otto's patrons sees him as "one of the last great individualists" (*Giving*, 185). McPhee, too, seems to admire Otto's distinct
individuality, but the writer appears to be most fascinated with the
chef's skill. When he describes Otto in action, McPhee's prose fairly
crackles with life: "[Otto] rocks a knife through some scallions, hauls a
grouper out of storage and begins to reduce it to fillets. He eats some
scallions and, slipping a hand into the refrigerator, pops a couple of
shrimp and two or three fresh scallops" (200). Otto *rocks, hauls,* and *pops*
as he performs his work. He is an artist—because of his great skill but
also because he is completely at home in his work. How he works *is* how
he lives. Even something as simple as making a hamburger becomes for
Otto a defining moment:

> He removed from the refrigerator the hundredth part of a ton of beef,
> sliced off a portion, put the rest of the meat back in the cooler, and
> returned to his working block, where his wrist began to flutter heavily,
> and in thirty seconds he had disassembled the chunk of beef and
> rearranged it as an oval patty. He ate some of the meat as he worked.
> Fast as it all happened, the cutting was done in three phases. He began in
> a one-handed rocking motion, and then held down the point of the knife
> with his left hand while pumping the handle with his right. He ended
> with a chopping motion, as if the knife were a hatchet. . . . He cooked
> the hamburger, turning it, touching it, turning it again and again, using
> the knife as a spatula. (192–3)

McPhee, like the subjects of his profiles, loves to analyze the physical
activity—be it a hook shot or the making of a hamburger. Otto is a master at what he does—repeating moves he has done over and over again
for years until his genius rests in his ability to do things precisely, artfully
without even thinking about them. As his wife says, it is his ability "to
juggle things in his head in the course of an evening . . . that is the differ-

ence between a chef and a cook" (230). Otto works in the "purity of his little inner sanctum" (247) making quenelles of veal and paella a la marinera. McPhee sits off to the side and watches the artist at work:

> A quarter to eight, and the china is rattling. Pot lids are spinning on the floor. The oven is up to four-fifty. Otto is moving so fast his work has become a collage of itself, as—all in a minute—he pours out lime juice, eats a handful of seviche, tosses a veal into a skillet, and hunts through the wild mushrooms for deposits of grit. Chaos cannot get at him in the depths of composition. Those are finished compositions going out through the door—the mottled brown envelopes of pork loin, the drapefold saucing of the poached quenelles. He is not only cooking. He works on all levels of the kitchen. (255)

As he moves through the kitchen, doing the work he loves, "a hobby that pays you" (254), Otto performs his magic and McPhee reports back to his readers, giving them all that the nonfiction writer can give in a human portrait—the words, the deeds, occasionally the thoughts that a subject will share. And Otto's wife, Anne, may be voicing something close to McPhee's philosophy when she says, "People are unknowable. They show you what you want to see. He [Otto] is a very honest person. Basically. In his bones. And that's what the food is all about" (261).

Levels of the Game

Generally, for the nonfiction writer, people are knowable only in their words and actions. Thoughts are a bit more difficult to come by in the process of reporting. In *Levels of the Game,* published in 1969, McPhee used an innovative approach in an attempt to reach another level in nonfiction characterization. Technically, McPhee used the point-by-point analysis of the match that he did with Arthur Ashe and Clark Graebner to create a narrative flow back and forth across the net, describing each player's shots and thoughts. He did much more reporting than that, though. He interviewed parents, friends, former coaches, wives. With the information he gathered, he flashes back into the players' lives at crucial moments in the match. Biography and athletic contest, then, play off of one another, giving the reader a deeper understanding of both players and the event, making it a portrait that plays on a number of different levels.

Levels of the Game was something of a conscious departure for McPhee. After writing about Bradley, Boyden, Hoving, and Gibbons, he felt that

he was becoming a bit jaded.[17] So, he opted to do two profiles in one,
letting one intersect with the other and become inter-reflective. As
McPhee saw the project, one plus one would equal a lot more than two:

> I thought about this for years. An actor and a director. An architect and
> some bull-headed client, prominent in some other field. A dancer and a
> choreographer. A ballplayer and a manager. So then one day I was look-
> ing at the semifinals of the U.S. Open Tennis Championship on CBS.
> There were Arthur Ashe and Clark Graebner playing against each other.
> They're both twenty-five years old, they're both Americans, one's white,
> one's black, and they would have known each other since they were
> eleven. And so that's where *Levels of the Game* came from. The basic tool
> in that piece was the tape of that television performance. . . . Without
> them [the tapes of the game] I couldn't have done it.[18]

McPhee's goal was to step outside the boundaries of the typical profile, to move beyond the kinds of profiles that he had been writing. In
many ways, he accomplished his goal in *Levels of the Game*. The word *levels* suggests a variety of possibilities in the context of the story. It points
to the varying levels of talent that one can find in the game of tennis,
and it suggests the level of brilliance that must be mastered to reach the
semifinals of the U.S. Open. Implicitly, it emphasizes the fact that an
excellent player can raise his level of play to greatness as Ashe does in
the last set of the match. The word *levels* is more suggestive than that,
however. The word turns back on the profile itself, commenting on the
possibilities inherent in the form. Human beings, as Otto's wife said,
may be ultimately unknowable, but in this story McPhee strives to see
his characters on more levels than he has previously. He shows them in
the past and the present, talking and thinking, feeling and analyzing.
He shows them under duress, because a sports contest like this one does
not build character but, as John Wooden, the former UCLA basketball
coach, once said, it reveals it. This is also a picture of different levels in
American society. It is not just black versus white. It is middle-class citizen versus the plutocrat. It is a clash of ideologies, liberal versus conservative, Democrat against Republican. It is a knight of change encountering a defender of the status quo.

None of the political or sociological implications, however, break the
flow of the narrative or detract from the tense drama of the match. The
paragraphs of personal history enhance the narrative by giving shape
and motive to Ashe's or Graebner's moves. In addition, such paragraphs
draw out the line of suspense. The background on each player's life and

philosophy makes them more than players: They become individuals that the reader cares about, and this makes the contest more significant. As McPhee describes them, Clark Graebner and Arthur Ashe seem to be ready-made antagonists. Although they play together on the U.S. Davis Cup team, they are precise opposites, it seems. Ashe has been brought up strictly by his axiomatic father. He had a specific curfew, and when he went off as a young boy to develop his tennis skills at Dr. Johnson's in Lynchburg, Virginia, he had to work for his keep. Graebner has been spoiled by his overindulgent parents, who have rented a junior high school for his private tennis lessons and who gave him unrestricted use of the family car. Graebner is often emotional on the court, losing his temper at linesmen or ball boys. Ashe is always in control. Each player has a definite view of the other's style of play. About Graebner's game, McPhee quotes Ashe saying, "He plays stiff, compact, Republican tennis. He's a damned smart player, a good thinker, but not a limber and flexible thinker. His game is predictable, but he has a sounder volley than I have, and a better forehand—more touch, more power" (*Levels,* 90). About Ashe, McPhee quotes Graebner's remark, "He plays the game with the lackadaisical, haphazard mannerisms of a liberal. He's an underprivileged type who worked his way up. . . . He gets looser and more liberal with the shots he tries, and pretty soon he is hitting shots everywhere" (93).

McPhee suggests that Graebner sees himself as a "Greek tragic hero always getting pushed around by the gods" (95), and Ashe seems somewhat reluctant to take on the role of leader of his people. Although Ashe is both reserved and conservative in his own way, by comparison to Graebner, he seems to be thoughtful and profoundly aware of his responsibilities in the world. Graebner's dream for his life after tennis is to be a millionaire by the time he is forty years old, to be a member of the River Club, live in Scarsdale, see his kids go to Vassar and Williams, watch his wife perform her duties in the Junior League, and spend his time on the board of Saxon Industries. Ashe's vision, on and off the court, is far deeper and more wide ranging than Graebner's, and if, as tennis player Charlie Pasarell observed, "tennis is a fight of character" (116), then it seems dramatically appropriate that Ashe is able to "level things," to strip away the edge that money and position may grant Graebner and raise his game to another plateau. When the last shot has been made, Ashe stands on his toes, "his arms flung open, wide, high" (150). In the "fight of character," McPhee implies, Ashe just has more than his opponent.

In *Levels of the Game,* McPhee goes beyond hagiography. He is fair and balanced in his portrayal of Ashe and Graebner, but in his own words and in those of Graebner's wife and friends, Graebner shows himself to be shallow and bigoted, at times. Ashe may seem a touch too cool at times, but he has learned how "to put some heart into many things" (117). Ashe has put his heart into the game, and in the process he has gained some perspective on life, as well.

Encounters with the Archdruid

In 1971, two years after *Levels of the Game,* McPhee published *Encounters with the Archdruid,* another gamble on his part to extend the boundaries of the profile form even further. This time he extended the possibilities by writing about three people all relating to a fourth. He was not sure what the theme would become or who the participants would be. Eventually, McPhee decided to write about David Brower, "the feistiest environmentalist," and three intelligent, articulate individuals who had pro-development philosophies.[19] One could guess that McPhee admires environmentalists like David Brower, but his account of Brower's three encounters with developers is written with novelistic skill, leaving the reader to make any political decisions. Even questions of character are left to the reader to answer. McPhee offers the basic facts about the various characters' lives, he lets them speak, he shows them act, but he does not so much create heroes (as he may have done in previous profiles) as he creates characters in a complex human drama.

McPhee's position as the literary reporter in *Encounters with the Archdruid* is one of firm impartiality, allowing each character to show his own story. The book is divided into three parts: "A Mountain," "An Island," and "A River." Each part positions David Brower, former head of the Sierra Club and leader of a conservation organization called Friends of the Earth, against one of his philosophical adversaries in a natural setting that is an environmental battleground. A sort of contest ensues, not unlike a semifinals match at the U.S. Open, and character is revealed. Even Brower, the ostensible hero of the story, is shown to have many contours to his character.

In the first section, "A Mountain," in which Brower hikes with Charles Park, a geologist and mineralogist, in the Glacier Peak Wilderness mountains, there appears to be no simple villain or hero. Park wants to mine the mountains. He is a man who believes "that if copper were to be found under the White House, the White House should be moved" (*Encounters,* 5). But he is also a geologist who goes into the field "because of love of the earth and the out-of-doors" (55). He is a man, McPhee says, "who knows what he is looking at in the wild country. I have never spent time with anyone who was more aware of the natural world" (67). As opposed to Brower, though, Park thinks principally in terms of practicality, not aesthetics. He is pragmatic, not spiritual. It is Brower who is linked symbolically with the mountain, a man who could be set down at night anywhere in the Sierra Nevada and in the morning light know exactly where he was. It is Park who gets satisfaction chipping away at the mountain, swinging at outcroppings with his pick. When McPhee asks him what he is looking for, Park grins and says, "Nothing, I just haven't hit one in a long time" (18). He is a man who loves the outdoors, but he also wants the wilderness to supply people's needs. "We need to lumber," he says. "We need to mine" (67).

McPhee takes no editorial stance on environmental issues in *Encounters with the Archdruid,* but at times in the narrative he does seem to lean in one direction or another. His sympathies seem to be with Brower in the first encounter, which ends with a picture of Brower's generosity and spirituality and of Park's materialism. They sit resting on Miner's Ridge, Park eating blueberries straight from the bush and Brower gathering his in a cup. "Brower's cup was up to its brim, and before he ate any himself he passed them among the rest of us. It was a curious and surpassingly generous gesture, since we were surrounded by bushes that were loaded with berries. We all accepted. 'I just feel sorry for all you people who don't know what these mountains are good for,' Brower said. 'What are they good for?' I asked. 'Berries,' said Brower. And Park said, 'Copper.' (75)" Park may have the last word, and he may be an attractive person, but it is Brower who has a sense of the possibilities of our companionship with the earth rather than our control of nature. Brower is a man whose "love of beauty is so powerful it leaps . . . [and] lands in unexpected places" (198).

In the next two sections of *Encounters with the Archdruid* McPhee narrates the story of Brower's meeting on Cumberland Island, off the coast of Georgia, with Charles Fraser, a real estate entrepreneur famed for the development of Sea Pines Plantation on Hilton Head; and his encounter with Floyd Dominy, Commissioner of the U.S. Bureau of Reclamation and arch-builder of dams, on a rafting trip through the Grand Canyon. Fraser, although a real estate developer, is something of a druid himself, a builder with a concern for the environment, and Brower wishes to take him into the fold. Brower's final words to his potential apostle Fraser are

"I have seen evidence of what you can do. Now make others do it"
(144).

More philosophical distance separates Floyd Dominy and Brower. As
McPhee protrays him, Dominy is an imposing figure, a scourge to conservationists, a man whose initials, F. E. D., seem more profoundly
appropriate than coincidence would allow. Brower is determined to see
the rivers in the United States run their natural course. Dominy, who
grew up in dry Western country and began his career building dams
seven feet high, eventually built dams over seven hundred feet high.
McPhee says Dominy would like to see "the Colorado River become a
series of large pools, one stepped above another, from the Mexican border to the Rocky Mountains, with the headwaters of each succeeding
lake lapping against the tailrace of a dam" (162).

The trip they take down the Colorado River is a confrontation
between giants, the Archdruid and the Devil, but McPhee presents
them as strong, well-meaning individuals who disagree about the wisdom, morality, and practicality of attempting to use nature for our own
purposes. Dominy, the Devil from the point of view of conservationists,
is portrayed as a heroic, undaunted, if at times arrogant, figure. Brower,
the religious leader of the conservation movement, is depicted as enig-
matically human. At one point in their journey down the river, Brower
decides not to run a rapid with the group. Dominy snarls contemptu-
ously, "The great outdoorsman!" When the raft glides to the shore at
the other end of the rapid, Dominy asks Brower why he did not ride
with them. "Because I'm chicken," Brower replies (231–2).

McPhee never analyzes Brower's fear or explains his actions. Rather,
he allows the structure of the narrative to make the comment. Immediately after Brower declares that he is "chicken," McPhee offers a biographical section describing Brower's scaling thirty-three peaks in the
Sierra Nevada. Then, he recounts Brower's and Dominy's conversation,
a dialogue by turns mocking, collegial, and angry. McPhee concludes
the story with a description of the group's negotiating the fearsome
Lava Falls. Right before they hit the drop, McPhee notices that Brower
is in the raft, hands tight on the safety rope, tendons taut in his neck.
But he is there. The narrative ends with the reader's admiration for
Brower's courage and character, but it ends with no clear winner in the
environmental debate. And, clearly, the battle will continue beyond this
encounter: "For a moment, we sat quietly in the calm, looking back.
Then Brower said, 'The foot of Lava Falls would be two hundred and
twenty-five feet beneath the surface of Lake Dominy.' Dominy said

nothing. He just sat there, drawing on a wet, dead cigar. Ten minutes later, however, in the dry and baking Arizona air, he struck a match and lighted the cigar again" (245).

Looking for a Ship

In 1990 McPhee wrote a book with what he felt was "the most complicated structure I ever got into."[20] On the surface, *Looking for a Ship* does not appear to be more complex structurally than *Levels of the Game* or *Encounters with the Archdruid*. It appears to follow an archetypal journey pattern. It is the story of a journey, the trip McPhee took with Andy Chase, a U.S. Merchant Marine officer. But, significantly, the journey and the ship that the two went on were, as McPhee once said, "completely randomly arrived at."[21] Initially, the structure of the piece was a gamble in which McPhee had to decide where the center of the story was (he decided that it was Valparaiso, Chile) and how to recount the events (he determined that a series of flashbacks with the Valparaiso episode as the fulcrum would work best). McPhee and his guide, Andy Chase, shipped out of Charleston, South Carolina, but it could have as easily been Jacksonville or New York City. Fate determined the ship they would get, the captain they would ship out with, and the itinerary the ship would follow. It so happened that the ship went from Charleston to Valparaiso, along the coast of South America and up to Port Newark.

At first, the story appears to be about Andy Chase and the deterioration of the Merchant Marine in the United States, but the structure of the story soon makes it apparent that Captain Paul McHenry Washburn, the skipper of the SS *Stella Lykes* and another of McPhee's skilled, rugged individualists, is closest to the heart of the story. Like Bradley or Hoving, Washburn not only loves his work and is expert at it, he is also eloquent when he speaks about his vocation. Simply, he is a fascinating man, as McPhee describes him: "Washburn will talk to anybody. If he sometimes seems to prefer talking to himself, there's an obvious reason: he's the most interesting person on the ship" (*Looking*, 40). Washburn is versatile enough to wax poetic about Rogers Hornsby or Christopher Columbus. He is a man of great intelligence and learning, but he did not have an easy time in school. With a Faulknerian sort of independent spirit, he got A's in the subjects he liked, but those he did not like, he simply did not study. He sees himself as a "maverick, an adventurer" (147). Placed in the context of his life, as McPhee recounts it, these words seem not egotistical but merely statements of fact. In the 1950s, when Washburn was thirteen, he started the first of his many personal vacations from formal schooling in Washington, D.C. As a teenager, he rode the rails as a hobo, joined a circus sideshow, and had an unpromising career as a prizefighter—then he shipped out on a banana boat headed for the Dominican Republic. In 1941, at the age of eighteen, he got his ordinary seaman's papers in the Merchant Marine. The only place Washburn ever felt that he fit, ever felt at home, was at sea.

McPhee is precise in describing Washburn's sense of vocation. At sea, Washburn has a sense of connection to everything around him. To him the boat is "a living thing" (59), and although he gets lost in his own driveway and needs his wife's navigational abilities to get him to the corner store when he is on land, on board ship he is a master, never lost or confused or uncertain. Similar to other McPhee characters, such as Bill Bradley or Frank Boyden, Washburn has an intuitive feel for his environment. He does not need to use the computerized satellite navigational system aboard the *Stella Lykes* because he "has an instinct for dead reckoning—the deduced reckoning of one's position from recorded course and speed" (119). McPhee makes it clear that Washburn does not romanticize the sea. It is his "twenty-four-hour-a-day sworn enemy" (127–8). But he would "rather be here for the worst that could be than over there [the land] for the best that could be there" (155). As it was for Ishmael and Huck Finn, the water is his escape. As he says, "If I made plans and they went wrong, I was gone—looking for a ship" (156).

Washburn, like the shipping company he works for and the U.S. Merchant Marine in general, seems to be a dying breed. As McPhee writes, "Among major American shipping companies, it [Lykes Brothers] seems to be competing with Sea-Land and American President Lines for that special form of venerability that is reserved for the last of anything. The last Mohican. The last passenger pigeon" (160–1). Washburn, like Andy Chase and many of the other crew members aboard the SS *Stella Lykes,* has been called to his profession, not unlike a Bradley or a Hoving or a Boyden had been called to theirs. These are men who take great pleasure and pride in what they do.

Of course, such descriptions of characters like Washburn or Andy Chase could teeter on the homiletic if it were not for McPhee's perfectly timed humor, a comic touch that can be found in all of his profiles. In *Looking for a Ship* the humor abounds, from his description of the look an attractive prostitute gave to the second mate—"The smile she threw at

Andy left his shadow on the deck" (226)—to his description of dinner aboard ship, a description that ranks with Melville's in *Moby Dick*. McPhee paints the scene this way:

> The captain was there, and Andy Chase, and Bernie Tibbotts. All three had been served and were eating. No one else was present. Tibbotts sat alone at a table, facing a wall. Chase sat alone at a table, facing the opposite wall. The captain, at his table, sat with his back to a third wall. . . . Franz Kafka was up in the ceiling, crawling on a fluorescent tube. No one spoke. No one so much as nodded when I came in. I sat down where I was supposed to: at a fourth table, across the room from the captain. I looked at him through the slot between the other men's backs. I did not have—I'm here to tell you—the temerity to speak. (205)

As McPhee makes clear in the course of the story, this is a happy ship and a friendly captain and crew, but this is not the world most of us are used to—this is a separate country and has its own set of customs.

"Travels in Georgia"

Most of McPhee's profiles examine a world of men, but there are a few exceptions. Every now and again, a woman enters this domain of builders, athletes, craftsmen, and adventurers. One of the most prominent examples is the story he wrote in 1973, "Travels in Georgia," which was included in the collection *Pieces of the Frame*. In that story Carol Ruckdeschel, a field zoologist from Atlanta, Georgia, guides McPhee around the state and introduces him to a memorable dining experience as well as a state that seems as much another country as Washburn's ocean.

"Travels in Georgia" is pure, undiluted McPhee. Edward Hoagland's analysis is illuminating: "He [McPhee] is most comfortable side by side with a chum rather than alone with his thoughts, but is preeminently a student of how people who are good at something do what they do: of craftsmanship, and people who in a private way thrive."[22] McPhee, the reporter, gravitates toward individuals he admires, people who are engaged passionately in their activities in the world, individuals who, like Thoreau, can live only one way—deliberately. In "Travels in Georgia," McPhee is among friends—Sam Candler, who made an appearance in *Encounters with the Archdruid*—and soul mates—Carol Ruckdeschel, who is as comfortable with rattlesnakes and snapping turtles in a Georgia swamp as she is eating grilled cheese sandwiches with Governor Jimmy Carter in his chandelier-lit dining room.

Both Sam and Carol teasingly refer to McPhee as "the little Yankee bastard," and the three of them share an expression that becomes a motif in the story—D.O.R., a phrase that stands for "Dead on the Road." At first, the phrase just describes the squirrels and snakes and possums that the three find along the road as they search within Georgia for specimens, foodstuffs, and wild places worth preserving. Along the way, the phrase takes on other meanings in the story. All sorts of D.O.R.s appear—a fan belt Sam mistakes for a snake, a banana peel Carol thinks is a jumping mouse, an abandoned gas station with rusting pumps, and a twenty-year-old Dodge on a back road, and even, outside the Newark Airport as the writer tries to escape civilization, "thousands and thousands of murmuring cars, moving nowhere, nowhere to move, shaking, vibrating, stinking, rattling, *Homo sapiens* D.O.R." (26). Hopping across fenders and crawling under trucks, McPhee escapes to the wilds of Georgia, and although he never becomes as comfortable with water moccasins as Carol is, he does seem content, a few hours after his escape from Newark, to be in the Georgia mountains eating a recently killed weasel.

Carol is something akin to a female Tarzan, as William Howarth describes her, "young, free, handsome, wild . . . [a woman who] fears no serpents, can live without men, takes things apart to see how they are made."[23] She is the epitome of the McPhee protagonist—capable, honest, resourceful. She is peculiarly and wonderfully individual. She is able to swiftly and efficiently dissect a snapping turtle, unsheathing her ever-ready hunting knife and slicing the flesh from the legs in thick strips of red meat. She coos over a dead possum, but she coolly breaks a double-edge razor blade lengthwise and with "a simple slice, she brought out the testicle . . . placed it on a sheet and measured it" (*Pieces*, 30). She loves the wild odor of game lifted warm from the roadside, but she acts as a sort of guardian angel to baby hawks, black widow spiders, rattlesnakes, and a dog called Catfish. With steely nerves she can squeeze the venom from a dead cottonmouth, but she often needs to hear a Johnny Cash song to lift her emotions during the day. And after McPhee describes Cash's singing ("He sounded as if he were smoking a peace pipe through an oboe" [38]), it may be easier for readers to understand her attraction to the music. She is a free spirit, something like one of Thoreau's "sojourners in civilized life." She lives simply and truly like a woman from another time, another place, barely touched by the motives and desires of the modern world.

But Carol is touched by the modern world, of course. In her search, along with Sam Candler, to find a way to keep the Chattahoochee River above Atlanta from becoming what it is like once it enters the boundaries of that city, Carol must engage in a political struggle. In an important respect, her whole life is a political struggle in her work for the Georgia Natural Areas Council, battling the push for new housing developments and new industries in wild areas. Before it hits the Atlanta area the Chattahoochee River is clear and wild, but once it passes into the city it is filled with thirty-five million gallons of partially treated sewage and forty million gallons of raw sewage every day. McPhee describes a trout caught near one of the power plants along the river: "It is difficult to imagine what sort of fin-rotted, five-legged, uranium-gilled, web-mouthed monster could live in the river by Georgia Power. Seen from the air (Sam showed it to me once in his plane), the spoiling of the Chattahoochee is instant, from river-water blue to sewer ochre-brown, as if a pair of colored ribbons had been sewn together there by the city" (53). McPhee ends the story with Sam, Carol, and himself taking a canoe trip down the Chattahoochee with a sympathetic Governor Jimmy Carter. But the concluding scene is in the governor's back yard, behind the mansion, where the group of them are shooting baskets. It is a lovely, enigmatic ending that reminds the reader that this is a slice of life, a piece of a journey, just a portion of Carol's story and only one moment in an ongoing and undecided struggle: "The Governor had the ball and was dribbling in place, as if contemplating a property owner in front of him, one-on-one. He went to the basket, shot, and missed. Carol got the rebound and fed the ball to Sam. He shot. He missed, too" (57).

The Survival of the Bark Canoe

Most of the subjects for McPhee's profiles fit the heroic pattern—they are model citizens, expert doers, called to a specific activity in the world, and able to eloquently explain their passions. In the final analysis, the general practitioners in "Heirs of General Practice" (published shortly after the death of McPhee's father), the basketball player turned senator in "Open Man," and the fiercely independent pioneers in Alaska appear to be exemplars. In this respect *The Survival of the Bark Canoe*, published in 1975, is an anomaly and Henri Vaillancourt is a sort of anti-hero or the typical McPhee hero turned inside out.

On the surface, Henri Vaillancourt, the central character of *The Survival of the Bark Canoe,* may seem to be a standard McPhee protagonist. He is an artisan without peer, a man who makes seven bark canoes a year, employing the methods that the Indians once used. The thwarts he makes from hardwood, the ribs from cedar, sewing them and lashing them with the split roots of pine, and the skeleton he covers with the strong and waterproof skin of white birch bark. He does not use power tools or even nails. Basically, he uses an axe, an awl, and a crooked knife to make his *objets d'art*—for he is an artist, as McPhee says, "with a historical purpose" (*Survival,* 25).

Like most of McPhee's artist-heroes, Vaillancourt is not so much an aesthete as he is a practical artist. The "artists" that McPhee writes about can be philosophical and intellectual, but there is a strong practical streak that runs throughout their activity, whatever it is. McPhee sees Vaillancourt as an artist by style and temperament. (53) And McPhee sees Vaillancourt's canoes as works of art: "Two were there when I first saw the yard. Their bark, smooth and taut, was of differing shades of brown, trellised with dark seams. . . . These things, to the eye, were perfect in their symmetry. Their color was pleasing. Turn them over—their ribs, thwarts, and planking suggested cabinetwork. Their authenticity seemed built in, sewed in, lashed in, undeniable. In the sunlight of that cold November morning, they were the two most beautiful canoes I had ever seen" (10–1). McPhee could as well be describing pieces of sculpture as canoes. Vaillancourt sells his works of art, but like most artists, he is "ferociously proprietary about them" (8). He likes to keep them around his shop in Greenville, New Hampshire, for as long as he can before he ships them out to the people who ordered them, and "his profoundest hope is that [the canoe] will survive its owner and then be passed on to a museum" (8).

Vaillancourt's aim is to build the perfect bark canoe. He built his first canoe at age fifteen, even though he had never ridden in one. Now, at twenty-five, he has a Hemingwayesque sort of artistic hubris: "With a singleness of purpose that defeats distraction, Henri Vaillancourt has appointed himself the keeper of this art. He has visited almost all the other living bark-canoe makers, and he has learned certain things from the Indians. He has returned home believing, though, that he is the most skillful of them all" (5). Beneath the patina of craftsman-like devotion to his work is another aspect of Vaillancourt's character, an obsessiveness that limits his vision of the world. McPhee's heroes are generally people whose obsessions bring them into the world and broaden and deepen their insight. In Vaillancourt's case, his art separates him from the community of men. Like a character in a Hawthorne short story, he seems to value his knowledge over his connection to people. As McPhee tells us about Vaillancourt, "So he went home to Greenville [after college] and began what in all likelihood will prove to be a life's career, since he appears to be interested in almost nothing else. Nothing much else enters his time, his thought, or his conversation that does not have to do with the making and use of birch-bark canoes" (7).

Before McPhee moves one-fifth of the way into the profile, he begins to recount the canoe trip that Vaillancourt, he, and three others took in the Penobscot-Allagash area of northern Maine. Very quickly Vaillancourt's true character, one only hinted at in the opening description of his artistry, begins to surface. He proves himself to be inconsiderate, dictatorial, rigid, and humorless. In contrast to David Brower in *Encounters with the Archdruid*, who shares his blueberries with everyone around him, Vaillancourt insists that everyone bring his own food: "He says that on one canoe trip he made he tried eating the communal way but 'that was a real bummer; someone always ate all the food,' and he will never do it again" (24). A canoe trip, as McPhee says, is "simply a rite of oneness with a certain terrain" (25), and in the course of the journey Vaillancourt demonstrates what he truly feels about nature and human companionship, as well.

In terms of the structure of the narrative, Vaillancourt's unattractive personality presented McPhee with problems. To be honest to his true view of Vaillancourt, McPhee had to sketch him as he had seen him, but he also realized that the canoe maker's unpleasant character would block most readers' admiration for his craft; it might even destroy a reader's interest in following such an unsympathetic character's story. Therefore, although McPhee typically structures such journey narratives as flashbacks, beginning somewhere in the middle of the trip and turning back at an appropriate point to the main character's life, he chose to begin, in a sense, with his first view of Vaillancourt as an accomplished craftsman. As McPhee said in an interview, "The first seven thousand words of it . . . describes him in his shop in Greenville, the person I got interested in, the person I went up there to watch making things. And then comes the canoe trip in chronological sequence. . . ."[24]

The canoe trip gives McPhee the opportunity to dramatize Vaillancourt's character, but it also gives him a chance to observe nature and ponder some lines from *The Maine Woods*, Thoreau's account of a canoe trip through the same area over one hundred years before. Much of

Maine is still wilderness. "There is more to Maine," McPhee says, "than exists in the imagination" (29). Maine is as big as all the other New England states put together, and the wilderness that Thoreau saw in the nineteenth century looks much the same to McPhee. It is the sort of environment that gave Thoreau the opportunity to *see,* and it affords McPhee the same benefit. He had hoped to see a moose (which he finally does, the animal ironically being chased by the glaring lights of a logging truck), but he seems satisfied to pause over the strange beauties of a loon:

> He is out there cruising still, in the spiralling morning mist, looking for fish, trolling. He trolls with his eyes. Water streams across his forehead as he moves along, and he holds his eyes just below the surface, watching the interior of the lake. . . . Now his body is up again, and he laughs. If the laugh were human, it would be a laugh of the deeply insane. The bird's lower jaw opens and claps shut five times in each laugh. . . . His back, in summer, is a tessellation of white squares and dots on a black field. His head is black and forest green, and so is his neck, which is sur-rounded with vertical white stripes. His eyes are red. In the air, he could be part flamingo—long neck extended, feet behind, back humped. (29–31)

For three pages and again later in the narrative he pauses to watch the loon, describing it with a musing and poetic eye. His willingness to hold still and observe during the course of the journey places McPhee in direct contrast to Vaillancourt, who seems to have little aesthetic sense or interest in the natural world: "The great beauty of the lake appar-ently means nothing to him [Vaillancourt]. He has worked for two days to get to it, and now wants to rush across it and portage away from it in the dusk and dark" (106). Vaillancourt proves to be impatient, selfish, and vain. He wolfs down more than his share of fresh water clams, he spends an inordinate amount of time combing his hair, and he allows others to carry his fair load in portages. Unlike other McPhee characters like Bill Bradley, Vaillancourt has not more than a modicum of interest in the people around him—he is consumed by his craft.

McPhee, a craftsman too, recognizes something of himself in Vaillan-court. Describing his love of the journey, McPhee says, "I like the pur-pose in the motion, the clear possession of a course to follow, the sense of the journey. I like to go to sleep early and rise with the sun. In these respects, I guess, I am much like Henri" (102). But, significantly, McPhee is a lover of digressions, moved to asides by the attraction of new things, interesting people, curious animals, plant life, rocks. To Henri Vaillancourt the world means only one thing—and he finds that in his bark canoes. To McPhee, and many of the people he writes about, the world, as it does for Browning's Fra Lippo Lippi, "means intensely, and means good."

McPhee finds much beauty and laughter in the world. His own cherishing of the things in nature acts as counterpoint to Vaillancourt's myopia. McPhee's self-deprecating humor, detailing his mishaps as a white-water canoeist, for example, highlights Vaillancourt's egotism and narrow view of the world. For Vaillancourt, much of the world is simply a "bummer."

The excursion is Vaillancourt's first long canoe trip, but the same is true for McPhee's friend Warren. It is not Vaillancourt's greenness, his lack of skill or judgment in certain circumstances, that make him so unsympathetic. It is his arrogance in the face of others' views, his indifference toward much of the natural world, the fact that his talent has done nothing, it seems, to humble him in relation to beauty, that makes him the inverse of the typical McPhee protagonist. Like most of his protagonists, McPhee understands the satisfactions that come from the making of things, from doing something well. In speaking about the rewards of writing, for instance, he has said, "Making something that you have a compulsion to make and being glad when it's done is a genuine pleasure. At least a few months later you're glad. The biggest reward for me is that those books of mine exist. I'm still a little bit surprised and awfully pleased that people seem to like them" (Personal Interview). A sense of humility and a balanced perspective are integral parts of the craftsman's pride in the work he has done. What the reader misses in Henri Vaillancourt's story is a protagonist, like Captain Washburn, who has a sense of where he is, or the wisdom to admit it and even laugh at himself when he gets lost in his own driveway.

The Ransom of Russian Art

With the publication of *The Ransom of Russian Art* in 1994, McPhee seems to have come full circle, writing a profile of a figure cut from the same mold as a Bradley, a Boyden, or a Hoving. In a review of the book, David Remnick astutely said, "McPhee's latest work, *The Ransom of*

Russian Art, a profile of an eccentric art collector, has the same qualities
of precision and praise as in *A Sense of Where You Are.* Norton Townsend
Dodge is an American original, an eccentric loaded with advanced
degrees in Russian studies and a gilded stock portfolio."[25] Unquestion-
ably, Norton Dodge is an eccentric. McPhee has the knack of finding, if
not his character's eccentricities, the unique traits in his subjects that
make them distinctive, individual. He may be writing about representative figures, but they are always sharply drawn individuals. First of all,
Dodge is unusual, with his "great odobene mustache" and his unkempt
demeanor—"Various friends likened him to an unmade bed" (*Ransom,*
8). He is the prototypical absent-minded professor, having to call a lock-
smith "to come and get him out of a situation that could have been alle-
viated by a key he later found in his pocket" (8). He is an Olympian
talker, as easy to interview as "the chips in a computer" (109). As
McPhee says, Dodge free associates and gives seventeen answers to one
question, "sixteen of them to questions you had not thought to ask"
(109). With a Mr. Magoo–like aplomb, he drives his car while reading
the newspaper, funnies first, or he writes his lecture notes for the college
classes he is teaching. He is blind in one eye, and his wife often asks him
which eye he has open when he is on the highway. He cannot find his
way out of the St. Louis airport, but he was able to negotiate the unlit
streets of Leningrad as he searched for dissident art from the 1950s until
the late 1970s.

    And this is really the heart of Dodge's story—his collecting of non-
conformist Russian art for three decades. By 1986, he had the largest
and most exhaustive collection of this art in the world. He spent more
than three million dollars on over nine thousand works of art, paintings
and sculpture, representing more than six hundred artists. Dodge's story
is the tale of the most unlikely of smugglers. He looks and acts more
like Oliver Hardy than James Bond, but nevertheless he was the man
who, according to the art critic Victor Tupitsyn, "singlehandedly saved
contemporary Russian art from total oblivion" (16).

    With his bald head and his walrus mustache, Dodge may have been a
less conspicuous figure in the Orwellian landscape of pre-glasnost Russia
than he would have been on the streets of the United States, but there is
no question about the danger involved in his chosen obsession. And
although the reviewer for the *New York Times Book Review* complained that
we never find out why Dodge did what he did, McPhee clearly suggests
that a few motives—a revulsion for totalitarianism, a love of art, and a
sympathy for the oppressed—are at work in Dodge simultaneously.[26]

Running a parallel narrative line to the story of Dodge's smuggling is the story of Evgeny Rukhin, a Russian artist of the first order and a courageous iconoclast whose passionately lived life and mysterious death serve as an informative backdrop to Dodge's seemingly charmed existence. More than likely, Rukhin was killed by the KGB. Dodge, too, could have been killed or imprisoned is the dramatic implication.

The last image that McPhee gives the reader is of Dodge in the apartment of the artist Alexander Shnurov in New York City after the fall of communism in Russia. Dodge coaxes McPhee into buying a hand-painted T-shirt, and then he gives the artist about one thousand dollars in fifty and hundred dollar bills. A gust of wind from a fan sends the bills flying around the room "like leaflets in the wind," but Dodge seems unconcerned (181). It is the artist and the work that he cares about, and with an American sense of insouciance he seems to trust in the goodness of the future and his ability to help shape it.

All of McPhee's heroes secure their individuality in the world of work—prospecting for gold, searching for wild areas to preserve, picking oranges, smuggling art. They are men and women of action. Experience is primary in McPhee's world. It is not a region populated by hedonists. The men and women he writes about are devoted to their callings—to the ships they sail on, the children in their charge, the gourmet meals they create. Work in McPhee's stories, as James Stull has pointed out, "constitutes a secular religion."[27] The saints that he portrays are often ordinary men and women who find their spirituality, their authenticity, in the work they do. Typically in his stories, work connects people to the larger world, often to nature. Usually, McPhee's heroes are immersed in their jobs, as he is immersed in the act of writing about them. They are precise craftspeople, as he is. In a world filled with cynicism and violence, he offers a transcendentalist vision akin to Emerson's and Thoreau's. His work dramatically argues that ordinary men and women of spirit and substance exist today, that the individual character has not been homogenized, that not all sense of place has been lost to urban sprawl.

Finally, many of McPhee's portraits are subtle autobiographies. This does not mean that he often focuses on his own life in his writing. Far from it, he is one of the most self-effacing of the literary journalists. But the characters he writes about are reflections of the traits he admires—skill, a sense of humor, a balanced perspective, a deep devotion to some work, a quirky individuality, an engagement with the natural world—all traits that he has in full measure.

McPhee's Other Self and "North of the C.P. Line"

At times, McPhee's characters become his Doppelgangers; Bill Bradley plays basketball, Henri Vaillancourt loves canoes, Euell Gibbons reads the land as if it were a text. But, perhaps, the most striking alter ego comes in the protagonist in the story "North of the C.P. Line," which is included in the collection *Table of Contents*. In the opening of that story about a north woods fish-and-game warden, McPhee explicitly discusses the sympathetic other self in his work: "There is a lot of identification, even transformation, in the work I do—moving along from place to place, person to person, as a reporter, a writer, repeatedly trying to sense another existence and in some ways share it. Never had that been more true than now, in part because he [the warden] was sitting there with my life in his hands while placing (in another way) his life in mine" (*Table*, 249). The fish-and-game warden, whose name happens to be John McPhee, is flying a plane over a lake in Maine, and the writer John McPhee is recording the details for a profile. Each man is in a vulnerable position. The game warden is literally and figuratively McPhee's "other self." The game warden is a man of knowledge and skill, a man vitally connected to the natural world around him. In drawing his portrait, McPhee draws a picture of himself:

> Whenever I think about him, however, I feel such a strong sense of iden-
> tification that I wonder if it is not a touch of envy—an ancestral form of
> envy, a benign and wistful envy, innocent of chagrin. As anyone might, I
> wish I knew what he knows—and wish not merely for his knowledge but
> for his compatibility with the backcountry and everything that lives
> there. I envy him his world, I suppose, in the way that one is sometimes
> drawn to be another person or live the life of a character encountered in a
> fiction. Time and again, when I think of him, and such thoughts start
> running through my mind, I invariably find myself wishing that I were
> John McPhee. (292–3)

The stories that McPhee has written over the past three decades, the profiles of ordinary but ideal Americans—self-reliant, articulate, and adept; their vocations making them more human rather than less so— have all along been part of his pastoral vision of the world. For McPhee, this world does exist, for he discovers it as a reporter in New Jersey or Alaska or on a small island west of the Scottish mainland. And the people who live in these worlds preserve the ideals of independence and craftsmanship that McPhee values as a man and a writer.

Chapter Five

The Experience of Place

Just as John McPhee's books are filled with the stories of individuals, all different and distinct but all sharing important traits, much of his work focuses on place. A question whispers through the pages of his stories— in what kind of world, he seems to ask, will such fierce independence as we see in many of his subjects continue to thrive? The sense of where you are, which threads its way through many of his character portraits, is aligned closely to the experience of place. Fred Brown in *The Pine Barrens* always knows where he is going on those endless sand roads, and Donald Gibbie in *The Crofter and the Laird* knows exactly where on his island to find lobsters. For the men and women of frontier Alaska, to be without a sense of place can literally mean death. Without a sense of place, McPhee seems to suggest in many of his books, a person cannot have a true sense of self.

A sense of place in McPhee's books nearly always involves a sense of journey or escape, as well, for there is McPhee the traveler-adventurer encountering the men and women who act as his expert-guides. McPhee is the archetypal wayfarer, a traveler cut from the same cloth as the prototypical wanderers from Odysseus and Ishmael to Marco Polo and Mark Twain. McPhee's journeys, like theirs, are mythic ones—a departure, an initiation, and a return are always part of his pilgrimages. He is grounded in the genteel Princeton, and typically he ventures out into the wilder world—the snake-filled back roads of Georgia, the bear-haunted mountains of Alaska, the wind-swept lakes of northern Maine. His return always comes in the same form, a boon for readers and for himself—a story recounting his travels and the knowledge of people and the world he has returned to bring us. Travel, for McPhee the writer, is connected to the origins of the word, *travail,* work or ordeal, a suffering that brings some wisdom.

McPhee is the journalist-journeyer going out to discover something of value in the world, going out to discover new worlds or a new way of looking at the old ones. Surely, this makes McPhee part of an established tradition. As Eric J. Leed pointed out in his fascinating study *The Mind of the Traveler,* "Travelers—particularly before the modern era of print and electronic media—were a primary source of news and information about the outer world, and journalism begins in the journeys and journals of seventeenth-century travelers."[1] It is in motion that McPhee is both connected to the world and maintains a distance from it. The thrill of escape from the known (in his case, the ivy-covered serenity of Princeton) is patently American, echoing writers from Washington Irving to Saul Bellow. McPhee seems to sense that travel, as Albert Camus once said, brings us back to ourselves. Travel is a way of finding what is true in ourselves and the world around us. Typically, McPhee places himself in the role of the stranger. He is both acolyte and doubting student, watching, listening, and, to varying degrees, participating in the worlds he encounters in his journeys. Often, McPhee finds the new and unexpected in a time in history when it seems almost impossible to find wildness or uniqueness in a world that is increasingly suburbanized and homogenized. "Travel," Eric Leed has said, "is no longer heroic or individualizing."[2] The traveler has become the tourist, one place can replace another, and in the process, it seems, the individual loses his or her sovereignty—unless, perhaps, the traveler, like John McPhee, sees clearly enough to find a world beyond the travel brochures and highway maps, a world that might be right in front of us if we would open our eyes to see it.

The Pine Barrens

In *The Pine Barrens,* published in 1968, McPhee offers what might be called his first profile of place. The Pine Barrens of New Jersey are a separate world, another country, and as Bill Wasovwich, one of the Pineys that McPhee meets, says, "There ain't no place like this left in the country, I don't believe—and I travelled around a little bit, too" (*Pine,* 13). The Pine Barrens are more like the back country of Mississippi than they are like Bayonne or Paterson. In the heart of the most densely populated state in the country sits a wilderness that hundreds of thousands of tourists pass through each year on their way to the shore or Atlantic City without ever noticing anything but a blur of trees.

From the first paragraph of the story, McPhee focuses the readers' attention on place. McPhee situates himself and his readers on an observation deck of the Bear Swamp Fire Tower, which allows a view of about twelve miles in any direction, a perspective that consists of serrated stands of white cedar, the ridges of low hills, shadowed streams, dwarf forests, lakes, cranberry bogs—in essence, hundreds of square miles of incongruous wilderness in the heart of the most infamously suburban and industrial state in the country. It is a "bewildering green country" (6) with a "fantastic ganglia" of sand roads (19). The population is as low as fifteen people per square mile in a state that has up to forty thousand people per square mile in some of its northern sections.

According to William Howarth, McPhee envisions the Pine Barrens as "a *locus classicus,* the place in America where cultural traditions of North and South meet."[3] The place is both paradigmatic and unique. It is an environment so at odds with the ordinary contemporary American experience that, paradoxically, it is emphatically American in its bristling individuality. McPhee spent about one year collecting information for his book on the Pine Barrens, taking trips of various lengths from his house in Princeton to the area, which is a short drive to the south. At first, after completing his research, McPhee felt stranded by the material. He came home from his last excursion into the Pine Barrens and spent two weeks in relative despair lying in his backyard trying to figure out how to organize the information. When he came upon the notion of having Fred Brown as the central character, the material took shape around him, the figure of independence and self-reliance (Personal Interview).

Frederick Chambers Brown is an embodiment of the Pine Barrens. He fits into this "distinct and separate world" (42) in a manner in which it is difficult to imagine him fitting into mainstream American society. More than one hundred years before McPhee wrote *The Pine Barrens,* an article in *Atlantic* magazine described the separateness of the place: "It is a region aboriginal in savagery, grand in the aspects of untrammelled Nature; where forests extend in uninterrupted lines over scores of miles; where we may wander a good day's journey without meeting half-a-dozen human faces; where stately deer will bound across our path, and bears dispute our passage through the cedar-brakes; where, in a word, we may enjoy the undiluted essence, the perfect wildness, of woodland life" (*Pine,* 41). Residents of the Pine Barrens like Fred Brown (McPhee soon drops the Frederick Chambers as if to say this is not a suburban lord of the manor) must be versatile to survive in this place. They must truly have a sense of where they are. If not, they could readily find themselves dangerously lost in the hundreds of thousands of acres of uninhabited woods. Both Bill Wasovwich and Fred Brown roam the woods when they are not working, and through years of experience are able to distinguish one seemingly identical sand road from another. Most newcomers to the Pine Barrens need maps to be able to "see," but

Fred "always knew exactly where he was going. . . . No matter where we were—far up near Mt. Misery, in the northern part of the pines, or over in the western extremities of the Wharton Tract, or down in the southeast, near the Bass River—Fred kept calling out directions" (19).

One of the ultimate sins in such a country, it seems, is not to have a sense of your surroundings. In the typical Pine Barrens manner of saying something three times, Fred Brown explains the problem he has with one of the fire watchers in a nearby tower: "He don't know the woods. He don't know the woods. He don't know the woods. He don't know nothing. . . . I've gunned this part of the woods since I was ten years old. I know every foot of it here" (20). Ultimately, this is what McPhee, the wanderer in the woods, attempts to bring back for his readers—a knowledge of this odd and oddly American place. Subtly, McPhee shifts from the character of the people to the character of the place itself. From Fred Brown's offering of water ("That's God's water. Take all you want" [13]), McPhee moves the story to the aquifer that runs throughout the Pine Barrens. "The water of the Pine Barrens is soft and pure," he says (13). Like the people who live on the land, the water is a prodigious but vulnerable resource. The water in the area is one of the things that give it value to the urban centers surrounding it. Another is the uninhabited space, ripe for housing developments and jetports.

McPhee and residents like Bill and Fred are interested in other forms of value. For example, they are interested in the history of the place. Nostalgically, Bill wishes he was "back there" (22), and from his statement McPhee takes the narrative into the past, into the ghost towns that dot the area and the legends and history that give the people a common story and a sense of community. The past is violent but lyrical and magical, as well. It is a past peopled with pirates and smugglers and a variety of types of criminals. It is a place founded upon escape: "Getting—or staying—away from everybody is a criterion that apparently continues to mean as much to many of the people in the pines as it did to some of their forebears who first settled there" (23). It was an escape for deserting Hessian soldiers, tormented Tories, and fallen Quakers.

It became a place vibrating with legends—of monsters and heroes. The Jersey Devil became the supernatural equivalent of the Loch Ness monster. A tradition of serio-comic tall tales emerged, told by a "class of local Homers" (68) like Cracky Wainwright and Ander Bozarth. They tell the kind of tales that echo an American tradition from John Smith to Davy Crockett. A piney recounts this archetypal story: "I heard old Cracky Wainwright say he seen two black snakes come together, and they was both mad. He seen they was going to fight, so he stood and watched them. The one got ahold of the other one's tail and began to swallow it. And the other got ahold of the other one's tail and began to swallow *him*. He said they kept on fighting and swallowing one another until both snakes was swallowed. There wasn't *any* snake left at all" (69). It is a place where the real world vibrates with magic, a place that has its own brand of metaphor—fingerboards and apple palsy and sugar sand. It is not a place lost to the practical necessities, however. True pineys can distinguish hog huckleberries from sugar huckleberries. They know how to harvest cranberries and sphagnum moss. They can be pineballers or moonshiners. They are a group that is "not afraid to work and not afraid not to work" (89). They are an independent lot who can survive in a variety of ways but a group that seems determined to work to live and not the other way around. There are millions of blueberry bushes in the area, but it might not be uncommon for a piney to refuse to cut one down for a scientific researcher.

The residents of the Pine Barrens seem proud of their separateness and, for the most part, happy with the way they live. As McPhee says, "A visitor who stays awhile in the Pine Barrens soon feels that he is in another country, where attitudes and ambitions are at variance with the American norm. People who drive around in the pines and see houses like Fred Brown's, with tarpaper peeling from the walls, and automobiles overturned in the front yard, often decide, as they drive on, that they have just looked destitution in the face. I wouldn't call it that. I have yet to meet anyone living in the Pine Barrens who has in any way indicated envy of people who live elsewhere" (55). Most of the pineys are hard working, self-sufficient, and if at times they are outlaws, they are generally harmless ones, for example, poaching a deer out of season.

Along the way, though, they have gotten some bad press and an unfortunate reputation. In 1913 the psychological researcher Elizabeth Kite published a report titled "The Pineys," which studied some potential state welfare cases. The newspapers and politicians picked up the story , and the word "piney" became associated with imbeciles, incest, and degenerates. As McPhee says, "The result of all this was a stigma that has never worn off" (53). Many people in New Jersey still imagine the residents of the Pine Barrens to be "hostile and semi-literate" inhabitants of "dark backlands" (53). In contrast to this perception, however, McPhee shows a people who are gentle and in touch with their environment. The people have a communal memory of events. They have a shared experience. They have a knowledge of their world—the botany, the wildlife, the ubiquitous fires. *The Pine Barrens* is a carefully structured narrative, and McPhee frames the conclusion with a serious dramatic purpose. He ends the story with his meeting in the Pine Barrens with Herbert Smith, the planner of a mini-megalopolis, complete with the largest jetport on earth, in the heart of the Pinelands. The philosophical-political point that may have been moving soundlessly through a good portion of the story is now given voice. McPhee is fair in his presentation of Smith. The planner speaks his mind, and McPhee describes him as "a trim, likable, red-headed man in his forties" (151). Smith feels that planned development of the area will be much wiser than the spotty, exploitative development that will most certainly occur, he believes, in twenty years. McPhee lets Smith have his say, but the final image we are left with is the perimeter of the pines contracting (157). It evokes the emotion of a noose tightening around the place and the people; and Bill Wasovwich's voice, shy and soft, seems to reverberate from the beginning of the story—"It would be the end of these woods."

"The Search for Marvin Gardens"

In "The Search for Marvin Gardens," which is included in the collection *Pieces of the Frame,* McPhee investigates another New Jersey locale, this one in a post-apocalyptic state of decay. In the story he uses the frame of a monopoly game that he is playing with a friend to focus his roamings around Atlantic City. Edward Hoagland said that the story "is saved from being meretricious by its unexpected seriousness—he actually does 'Go to Jail.' "[4] What Hoagland fails to recognize, perhaps, is that "The Search for Marvin Gardens" is more than just a miniature tour de force; it announces its seriousness before the writer makes his several visits to the Atlantic City Jail. From the second sentence of the story, which describes packs of dogs that range along Vermont Avenue, the writer depicts a landscape that seems close to a scene from the film *Road Warrior.* It is a place reminiscent of a fictional description of a city seen in the aftermath of a nuclear war. It is filled with shattered glass, abandoned buildings, garbage-strewn streets. It could be, as the writer says, "Cologne in 1944" (*Pieces,* 81). As McPhee describes the town, "It is deep and complex decay. Roofs are off. Bricks are scattered in the street. People sit on porches, six deep, at nine on a Monday morning. . . . Between Mediterranean and Baltic runs a chain-link fence, enclosing rubble. A patrol car sits idling by the curb. In the back is a German shepherd. A sign on the fence says, 'Beware of Bad Dogs'" (81). Dogs drift everywhere amidst the garbage and rubble, and the entire landscape seems surreal. The premise of the story, surely, is clever; however, it is not cleverness that the reader is left with but rather a sense of a forgotten past, a lost innocence, and the nightmare of urban decay. Atlantic City has become a "salt-water ghetto" (86), and there is a considerable disparity between the game and the reality, between the past and the present. Where there were once mansions, there are now empty lots. Where there were once elm-lined residential streets, there are now loan offices and bars.

McPhee eventually finds Marvin Gardens, but it is not in Atlantic City. It is a secluded suburb, a sanctuary from the urban destruction, but it seems no more real than the surreal modern city or the game that has now only a literally nominal connection to the place it once was supposed to describe. "The Search for Marvin Gardens," by implication, yearns for the lost pastoral. In McPhee's story, no one can tell him where Marvin Gardens is, although many of the people he speaks with think that they have heard of it. Like many in the modern world they have little sense of place. Alienated, anesthetized by the noise, the pollution, and the violence they confront every day, these people may long, like many of McPhee's readers, perhaps, for other climes and another moment in history.

The Crofter and the Laird

In 1970, with *The Crofter and the Laird,* McPhee describes his ancestral home on Colonsay, an island twenty-five miles west of the Scottish mainland, and once again, as he did in *The Pine Barrens,* pictures an anomalous land that seems in ways wonderfully out of step with the modern world. Colonsay is another one of those places, like the New Jersey Pine Barrens, where the circle of civilization is tightening around it. In the case of Colonsay, it is an island of seventeen square miles of moor, outcropping, and mountain on which one hundred thirty-eight people live. Like the people of the Pine Barrens, the inhabitants of Colonsay are skilled in a variety of ways to survive on their island. The people *croft* (farm); they hunt for rabbits, pheasants, or wild goats; they collect mussels, clams, and lobsters; they search for the eggs of eider ducks and mallards; they make their own butter and cheese; they gather watercress by the streams and eat sea kale. Among other things, it is an "apparent affection for independence" (35) that keeps a crofter like Donald McNeill on his homeland even though he earns a precarious living, putting in seventy hours a week at the croft alone to make the equivalent of $1,500 a year. As McNeill says, "I'm quite happy here. I make out, so long as the shore's handy, and such like. But if you expect many things in life, crofting isn't the way to get them. Crofting cannot keep up with the times. Most people expect more than the bare necessities of living now. And crofting is not a livelihood. It's an existence" (*Crofter*, 35–6). It is also a way of life, an anachronism built on rock and legends and the intricate webbing of tradition. Colonsay, with its seventeen crofts and seven farms (any piece of property with more than forty-nine tillable acres), is a feudal society. The people who live on the island all rent their places from the *laird,* Euan Howard, the fourth Baron Strathcona, the absentee landlord who lives in Bath, England. It is an ancient system that has its roots in the battles between the clans and the English. It is encumbered by a history of ill feeling, fostered by broken oaths and pillage that is reminiscent of the treatment of native Americans in the nineteenth century in the United States.

The previous laird, Euan Howard's father, acted as a benevolent despot, responding to any claims for repairs or improvements that the tenants made. The new laird, however, is a modern businessman and treats the island as if it were a business that has not been run properly. He has a sincere affection for the place, but he will not run it at a loss. The rents, which are set by the Scottish Land Court, are low—lower in 1969 than they were in 1905. According to the new laird, when he inherited the island it was losing ten thousand pounds each year. He began to cut back, and the islanders did not like the new way of doing business. As Euan Howard sees it,

> It is not easy, or practical, to maintain a paradise. People complain about broken skylights and let the rain pour into their houses while they wait for the estate to repair the damage. . . . Colonsay has an ancient feudal society which basically wants to go on being feudal, provided they can find someone who wants to play at—and finance—being a feudal baron. The term "laird" is slightly fey and old-fashioned. I am the landlord and the proprietor. . . . The paternalistic and benevolent landlord cannot go on being as paternalistic and benevolent as he used to be, and this calls into question the viability of the whole community. (129–30)

McPhee never takes sides with the laird or the crofters. Both sides make sense, but as the debate reverberates throughout the book about how much the laird should be responsible for and how much the tides of the twentieth century can be stopped from encroaching on the shores of the island, the way of life seems to be endangered. Howard's cutbacks in coal and electricity combined with the lack of economic opportunity have led to an attrition that might eventually make Colonsay as much a memory as the history and legends that seem fixed in its cairns and caves. It is an island of one elementary school, one store, one pub, and two funerals for every marriage. Other nearby islands of Argyll, such as Pabay, Taransay, Scarba, and St. Kilda, were all once populated and now are uninhabited. In 1830 the population of Colonsay was one thousand. Before long, McPhee says, the population could be as low as seventy. "There is, at the moment, only one teen-age girl on the island, so dances are no longer held. There are only eight people whose ages are between fourteen and twenty-six. Among the older people there is a profound sense of unease about the future of Colonsay" (81–2).

Like a novelist, McPhee tells his story of gossip and legend, of independence and conflict, of bagpipers and peddlars, without ever providing an answer to the question of whether such an island seemingly outside the stream of time can continue to exist. Colonsay, as McPhee suggests, is a separate universe, "a small continent" where the people seem to be "masters, for a few pounds' rent a year, of considerable domains, with an independence that must go beyond any usual sense of that word elsewhere, except on another remote island. I have heard them say, with no note of daring or flippancy in their voices or of any doubt whatever, that there is nothing an incomer could teach an islander. In this world, it is true" (58).

By dramatic implication, McPhee may also be holding up his pastoral vision of the world as a contrast to the typical way people live in the modern times and be making a plaintive cry about the imminent loss of independent communities such as Colonsay. In 1969, when McPhee was writing *The Crofter and the Laird,* the news was focused on Vietnam and the massacre at Mai Lai. It was the age of Aquarius, and at Woodstock young people were trying to create an island of their own. *The Graduate* was depicting the materialism and confusion of a generation, and Norman Mailer's *The Armies of the Night,* which had loudly proclaimed its own importance, had received the Pulitzer Prize. In 1970, when *The Crofter and the Laird* was published, the nonfiction bestseller list was topped by *The Sensuous Woman* by "J" and *Everything You Wanted to Know about Sex* by Dr. Reuben. Within this context, in particular, perhaps, places like Colonsay are appealing anachronisms, small circles outside the drift of the present, more "lifeboat" than town, where things change slowly and events, such as the untimely demise of a chicken, make big news. Colonsay is the type of place where everyone knows what has happened almost as soon as the event occurs. It is a place filled with gossip, quick temper, and a Highland sense of humor. It is the kind of place where people still have the ability and the inclination, perhaps, to look at one another and see, for example, a handsome man with "a smile that can dry the rain before it hits the ground" (45).

It seems significant that McPhee concludes *The Crofter and the Laird* with a description of the legend that "hangs above the Hebrides more thickly than clouds" (133). The stories of seal women, elves, *glaistigs,* and seers that are embedded in the soil and the "Sith" ("the still folk," "the people of peace," "the silently moving people" [138]), connect the physical world to the supernatural one. "History proliferated into fantasy, and pure fantasy became history" (138). What part of Colonsay is worth saving, McPhee seems to ask, or will it soon all be transformed into ghosts and legends? Like his ancestor, a chief from Colonsay who performed the role of scribe at a parliament of the isles held on the island of Loch Finlagan, McPhee realizes that his task, simply and straightforwardly, is to record the story.

La Place de la Concorde Suisse

In 1984, McPhee examined another foreign landscape, Switzerland, in *La Place de la Concorde Suisse.* Outwardly, the subject seems an unusual one for McPhee—the Swiss Army. The military, like politics, seemed outside his sphere of interest; however, the Swiss Army is not a typical military institution. It is a militia of six hundred fifty thousand people in a country of under seven million. It is a civilian army, ready to mobilize in less than forty-eight hours. It is not so much the military that McPhee is examining in *La Place de la Concorde Suisse* as it is their very foreign-ness, their separation from the modern world. It is the individuality and uniqueness that absorbs his attention, and in this respect the story is similar to *The Pine Barrens* or *The Crofter and the Laird.*

Switzerland is a paradox: It has either the most pacific of warlike people or the most warlike of pacific cultures. It is a nation with the deeply held belief that its peacefulness and neutrality can only be preserved through military preparedness of the highest order. Through a warlike demeanor, the people believe, will come the absence of war. They seem to be the most civilized of people, the most cultivated soldiers. In the most awe-inspiring natural settings, they play their war games, Mont Blanc in one distance and the Weisshorn in another. The army is something like a democratic men's club. The soldiers train hard, but civilization is never far behind:

> Resting level on rock and snow, a table has been set, with a red tablecloth, and the sun—at half past nine—has come over the Torrenthorn to shine on silver platters of rolled shaved beef, bacon, sausages, wedges of tomato, half-sliced pickles in the shape of fans. Officers stand around the table. There is a company of teacups in close ranks, another of stemmed glassware. There are baskets of bread. The wines are of the Valais. The red is Chapelle de Salquenen. The rose is Œil de Perdix, in a bucket full of snow. Tschumy drinks a cup of tea. A promeneur happens by—a citizen in knickers, boots, heavy socks, a mountain hat—on his way from who knows to where. He just appears, like a genie. His appearance suggests that he is above fifty and done with the army. He absorbs the scene: the festive table, the officers sipping and nibbling and quietly debriefing, the soldiers at a distance sitting in clusters on their packs, the charcoal streaks on the exploded snow. "Gut," he says, and he waves and walks on. (*Place*, 9–10)

As the Swiss are likely to say, "Switzerland does not have an army, Switzerland is an army" (136). In a sense, the country is an island in the midst of Europe, and as much as the Swiss pride themselves on watch making, it is a country, in many respects, that is outside the influence of time. The Swiss have an idiosyncratic relationship to history and to their environment. They live in the modern world as bankers and lawyers and chemists, but they have assault rifles in their closets in case they are called upon to defend their country, even the Konkordiaplatz, the frozen intersection of glacial ice, known as La Place de la Concorde Suisse— "This place that will never need defending represents what the Swiss defend" (11).

What may have at first appeared to be an unusual subject for McPhee is actually a typical one for him—a story about an independent people who, in their quiet way, fight for their freedom. As one citizen says, the people are prepared to fight "even against the government if the government were to capitulate" (26). The Swiss Army that McPhee shows us is made up of bankers, farmers, lawyers. It is a democratic collection of individuals from all over the country, citizens who speak German or Italian or French. Leo Fassler is a foreman in a factory, Urs Marchy a salesman from Zurich, Sigward Strub a licensing manager for a pharmaceutical company in Basel, and Luc Massy a wine maker from Espesses. The army is a democratizing influence. "The Swiss school system tends to separate people from the age of twelve according to background, intelligence, and future profession. In the vital way that the American public high school draws together skeins of American society, the Swiss Army knits Switzerland" (99). Every soldier knows intimately the territory that he will defend. Each knows it as well as Donald McNeill knows the lobster caves on Colonsay. As on Colonsay or in the Pine Barrens, there is a sense of community and a shared heritage. Therefore, this little neutral country may be the perfect subject for McPhee's "Swiss-like attention to detail [in a] prose so precise as to allow the subject to shine through without obstruction."[5] While McPhee once again plays the scribe, standing a little apart, "rapidly writing notes" (142), the Swiss Army plays its war games with a great deal of good humor and panache and an equal amount of seriousness.

Coming into the Country

It is the American landscape, specifically the Alaskan frontier, that McPhee investigates in *Coming into the Country,* which was published in 1977. Many agree with Edward Hoagland's assessment of the work, that it is a "long, permanent book . . . a species of masterpiece."[6] It has a modern epic quality to it, with the requisite and often larger-than-life heroes, the vast setting, the deeds of great skill and courage, the simple yet literary style. Like most epics, *Coming into the Country* begins *in medias res,* with McPhee on a canoe and kayak trip on the Salmon River of the Brooks Range, the most northern of Alaska's nineteen streams carrying the appellation "Salmon." The watershed for this river is above the Arctic Circle, a place that seems as magical and faraway to most Americans as the dark side of the moon. McPhee, the nonfiction artist, recounts the stories of his Alaskan heroes with something close to the same balance and objectivity that the epic poet was once noted for using. McPhee, like Homer in *The Iliad,* offers his own type of catalogues—of people and equipment, of wild animals and mountain peaks. As much as Whitman's *Leaves of Grass* is an epic describing the generic American, *Coming into the Country* is an account of a profound aspect of the American spirit on the verge of extinction.

The Alaska that McPhee describes in *Coming into the Country* seems to be a separate country, as foreign as the islands off the coast of Scotland.[7] But Alaska, like the New Jersey Pine Barrens, is vitally and particularly

American in the sense of adventure it affords and the spirit of self-reliance it demands. "Alaska," as McPhee says, "is a foreign country significantly populated with Americans" (*Country*, 126). It is at once huge beyond the scope of the imagination and parochial in the strictest sense of the term:

> If Boston was once the most provincial place in America (the story goes that after a six-megaton bomb exploded in Times Square a headline in a Boston paper would say "Hub Man Killed in New York Blast"), Alaska, in this respect, may have replaced Boston. In Alaska, the conversation is Alaska. Alaskans, by and large, seem to know little and to say less about what is going on outside. They talk about their land, their bears, their fish, their rivers. They talk about subsistence hunting, forbidden hunting, and living in trespass. They have their own lexicon. A senior citizen is a pioneer, snow is termination dust, and the N.B.A. is the National Bank of Alaska. (126)

Alaska is an Aleut word that means "the great land," and it is a place that "runs off the edge of the imagination, with its tracklessness, its beyond-the-ridge-line surprises, its hundreds of millions of acres of wilderness" (133). It seems close to the last frontier on this planet for Americans. McPhee says that his pulse has quickened all of his life by the very sound of the word *wild* (271), and in describing his journey down the Salmon in book I of *Coming into the Country,* he pictures for his readers "the clearest and the wildest river" he had ever seen (73–4).

Coming into the Country is divided into three sections, each giving a different view of the seemingly boundless landscape. Book I, "The Encircled River," introduces the major issues of preservation versus development; book II, "What They Were Hunting For," portrays some of the politics in the state; and book III, "Coming into the Country," is by far the longest and comes to the heart of the story—the people who hunt and fish and make their lives in the wild land. Before introducing his readers to the people who have chosen to make their way in the country, McPhee first examines some of the paradoxes at the center of Alaskan life.

Book I, "The Encircled River," places McPhee with four men who are part of a state-federal study team trying to determine whether the Salmon should be part of the wild-river proposal before Congress, a proposal that would set aside the area as unalterable wild terrain. They are five of "perhaps a dozen outsiders [who] have travelled . . . in boats down the length of the river" (8). Like much of the state, it seems a congruous part of the "utter wilderness—uncompromising, unhuman wilderness" (108) that is Alaska. It is a landscape of wolf tracks and grizzly scat. As McPhee says, it is "in all likelihood, the most isolated wilderness I would ever see" (50). It is an immense land with a small population. It is open, inviting, threatening, beautiful, rugged, filled with wealth, dense with dangers. It is simple and incongruous at the same time. "What had struck me most in the isolation of the wilderness was an abiding sense of paradox. In its raw, convincing emphasis on the irrelevance of the visitor, it was forcefully, importantly repellent. It was no less strongly attractive—with a beauty of nowhere else, composed in turning circles. If the wild land was indifferent, it gave a sense of difference. If at moments it was frightening, requiring an effort to put down the conflagrationary imagination, it also augmented the touch of life. This was not a dare with nature. This was nature" (93). The rivers are clear, the animals abundant, the forests are a "perfect stillness" (27). It is a natural place "in balance with itself" (16), and the crucial question, one that McPhee announces early in the first section, is "what is to be the fate of all this land?" (18).

To a great extent, the sense of place comes from the sense of individual spirit with which the wilderness is imbued. The image of Alaska is nowhere more strikingly symbolized in *Coming into the Country* than it is in the grizzly bear. Bear stories enflame McPhee's imagination throughout the narrative. Bears are something to be feared, but they are also all that Alaska means. For McPhee, the grizzly implies a world; it is "an affirmation to the rest of the earth that this kind of place was extant" (63). The sight of the grizzly stirs him "like nothing else the country could contain" (62). McPhee admires their power and strength, he admires their dangerous wildness, their intelligence, their independence. He dreams of the grizzly at night. The bear, in color, stands on the side of a hill. It is a vision of Alaska, of a paradoxical place where the beauty would not exist without the threat, where the connection to nature comes in the difficult encounter with it. The bears suggest all that is dangerously alive and beautiful in the landscape. "If bears were no longer in the country," McPhee says, "I would not have come. I am here, in a sense, because they survive" (418). Toward the end of his adventure in Alaska, he has eaten grizzly steak, "a strange communion." He says, "I had chewed the flag, consumed the symbol of the total wild, and, from that meal forward, if a bear should ever wish to reciprocate, it would only be what I deserve" (421).

Alaska, like the grizzly, is brutal and magnificent. Like the grizzly, it is also endangered, vulnerable. Man and technology bring the most threat. The discovery of oil was like the discovery of gold. "Alaska suddenly had more development than it could absorb. It suddenly had manifold inflation and a glut of trailer parks. It had traffic jams. You could pick up a telephone and 'dial a date.' In the reasonably accessible bush, fishing and hunting—the sorts of things many people had long sought in Alaska—became crowded and poor" (84).

In 1971 the Alaska Native Claims Settlement Act gave a billion dollars and forty million acres to the sixty thousand natives of the state. This opened the way for the Trans-Alaska Pipeline, and conservationists' protests forced Congress to set aside some eighty million acres as national parks, national wildlife refuges, and wild rivers. The Alaskan debate hinges on the issue of development versus preservation, it seems, although McPhee comes up with an interesting twist on the discussion in the concluding pages of the book. There are those, like McPhee's friend John Kauffmann, who feel that at least one-fourth of the state should be kept as wilderness forever. Kauffmann feels that the "most inventive thing to do . . . was nothing. Let the land stand wild, without so much as a man-made trail" (83). Others, like Robert Atwood, the editor and publisher of the Anchorage *Times,* feel that Alaska should develop its resources and subordinate any preservationist's instincts to the national interest in oil sufficiency.

Caught amidst the differing viewpoints are the natives and the settlers in the state. One of the primary images in the first section of the book is the image of the circle, McPhee's circular journey along the Salmon and Kobuk Rivers, the cycles that are inherent in Alaskan life, even the salmon he views, "circling, an endless attention of rings" (7). In the cycles of the place, the Eskimos live in harmony with the natural geometry of Alaska. They are uncomfortable with the patterns imposed by politicians, with lands divided and subdivided for political and economic purposes. "Kobuk societies once functioned like the clans of Scotland. Terrain was common to all. Kinship patterned things; ownership did not. Use determined use. The sense of private property that has been jacketed upon them is . . . incompatible with subsistence harvesting and its changeful cycles" (35). Theirs is a true ecology, a natural connection to their environment, an accommodation with the cycles of fishing and hunting and gathering that the country and the seasons demand. When they hunt for caribou, for instance, they use the whole animal. "They eat the meat raw and in roasts and stews. They eat greens from the stomach, muscles from the jaw, fat from behind the eyes. The hide goes into certain winter clothing that nothing manufactured can equal" (33). The Kobuk Eskimos have expanded and contracted along the river lands over the centuries as the caribou have risen and fallen in natural cycles.

As McPhee describes his own river journey, his "closing a circuit, a hundred miles from the upper Salmon, where a helicopter took us, from Kiana, at the start" (40), he draws a picture of the native people of the land, a picture that could have come from Paul Gauguin, the French postimpressionist painter who is famous for his views of nineteenth-century Tahitian life. McPhee offers an idyllic miniature of the people of Kiana. As he waits for the plane to take him to Kotzebue, he falls asleep only to be awakened a short time later by the voices of children. Three little girls who had been picking blueberries on the other side of the runway stood by him, holding the berries along with hard candies and offering them to McPhee. "They asked for nothing. They were not shy. They were totally unself-conscious. . . . When they noticed my monocular, on a lanyard around my neck, they got down beside me, picked it off my chest, and spied on the town. They leaned over, one at a time, and put their noses down against mine, draping around my head their soft black hair. They stared into my eyes. Their eyes were dark and northern, in beautiful almond faces, aripple with smiles" (41–2). The scene is Edenic, the young girls more innocent and open than one can imagine their modern, media-trained counterparts in the lower Forty Eight to be.

McPhee concludes "The Encircled River" with the completion of his own narrative circle. "We drifted to the rip, and down it past the mutilated salmon. Then we came to another long flat surface, spraying up the light of the sun. My bandanna, around my head, was nearly dry. I took it off, and trailed it in the river" (95). Right before the final image of the bandanna, returning to the first line of the section, McPhee describes a sighting of a grizzly that playfully tosses a ten-pound salmon in the air, then like the archetypal American cowboy, twirls it over his head, "lariat salmon" (94). It is an image that suggests independence and power, the grizzly's brown fur rippling "like a field under wind" (95). McPhee suggests both the majesty and the threat when he says, "If we were looking at something we had rarely seen before, God help him so was he" (95). The threat is not so much from the bear, it seems, but from man. At the beginning of "The Encircled River" there was an image of circling salmon. At the end there is a mutilated corpse, as if to focus the reader's attention on man's entrance into paradise. Perhaps, there is a skillfully wrought melancholy note sounded in the final paragraph.

Ronald Weber believes that, intentionally or not, McPhee creates an ending that brings to mind Ernest Hemingway's "Indian Camp."[8] Weber is insightful to see the allusion to Hemingway's story, and more than likely McPhee was conscious of the connection. Hemingway's story ends with Nick Adams in the stern of a rowboat as his father rows them home after a traumatic night. "The sun was coming up over the hills. A bass jumped, making a circle in the water. Nick trailed his hand in the water. It felt warm in the sharp chill of the morning."[9] In the final paragraph of "The Encircled River," there are the sun, the fish, the hand trailing in the river.

The collection of images seems more than coincidental, for McPhee, particularly as a young writer, felt the influence of Hemingway. In his appendix to his undergraduate thesis at Princeton, McPhee responded angrily to Frost scholar Lawrance Thompson's suggestion that his work might be too much like Hemingway's in terms of his use of dialogue: "Lawrance Thompson has said cuttingly 'You've been influenced by Hemingway.' Besides feeling like a Buddhist who has been spit upon by Buddha, I was also annoyed. Now Hemingway's writing is clean and good and I like it very much. It has been known to move me, Scribner's, and even the earth. But I am surprised to hear that he has a monopoly on the dialogue method, although he employs it truly. And, parenthetically, I wonder how many writers have been told by Thompson that their work showed the influence of Shakespeare."[10] There is an unwonted, perhaps youthful, sarcasm in the passage. Clearly the twenty-one–year–old McPhee was no happier with Thompson's brand of literary criticism than Robert Frost would have been. There is even what amounts to a conscious parody of Hemingway in the language of McPhee's defense, but there is little question about his admiration for Hemingway's skill or his familiarity with his work.

In book II, "What They Were Hunting For," McPhee describes a helicopter trip he took with a committee charged with selecting the site for a new Alaskan capital. The site is to be moved from Juneau, on the eccentric southern peninsula and inaccessible by road, to an appropriate place that is at a certain distance from the competing interests in Fairbanks and Anchorage and ideally in view of Mt. McKinley, which the Indians call "Denali," the great one. During the course of the helicopter excursion, McPhee presents various ideas about Alaska's future through the voices of the committee members, along with his own interpretation of matters. There are heated commercial and political interests involved in the selection process, and the inspection trip reflects them. Certain factors—the presence of permafrost or the absence of roads and railroads—narrow the field of possibilities to the Susitna Valley, between the Alaska Range and Anchorage. McPhee makes it quite clear that the new capital should not be modeled on Fairbanks or Anchorage. Fairbanks has more motor vehicles per capita than Los Angeles, and because of the ice fog it has "an especially pernicious, carcinogenic subarctic variety of smog" (106). But Anchorage would be even worse. "Anchorage is not a frontier town. It is virtually unrelated to its environment. It has come in on the wind, an American spore. A large cookie cutter brought down on El Paso could lift something like Anchorage into the air. Anchorage is the northern rim of Trenton, the center of Oxnard, the ocean-blind precincts of Daytona Beach. It is condensed, instant Albuquerque" (130). This "portable Passaic" grew "like mold" (132–3).

There are one hundred eighty thousand people in Anchorage, seemingly trapped in an ugly urban prison as the wilderness lies a tantalizing but impossible distance beyond their reach, for the only way to get to it is by costly airplane or helicopter ride into the bush. There are wealthy sections of Anchorage where people live in heavy, substantial homes whose style is "American Dentist" (135). As McPhee says about these subdivisions, whole neighborhoods seem "to be struggling to remember Scarsdale. But not to find Alaska" (135). In its own character, with its own independent spirit, Alaska is distinctive. When it tries to be like the lower Forty Eight, the state creates cities that are simulacra, derivative, and disheartening. "Within such vastness, Anchorage is a mere pustule, a dot, a minim—a walled city, wild as Yonkers, with the wildlife riding in a hundred and ninety-three thousand trucks and cars" (133). For McPhee the most appealing, perhaps the only appealing, sight in Anchorage sits next to a gargantuan J. C. Penney complex in the downtown section—a group of weedy vacant lots with five log cabins on them, remnants of a world that was once there and has refused, by some stubborn logic, to budge. Anchorage is a typical American city, but Alaska is not typically American. At the conclusion of the second section of the book, McPhee mentions that of the three sites chosen by the committee the voters favor the one east of the hamlet of Willow, but the writer has already made the reader wonder in "What They Were Hunting For" if the hunter will not be caught in his own trap.

Book III, "Coming into the Country," is longer than the first two sections together. Whereas the first two sections present issues and ideas

more than character sketches, the third section dramatizes the stories of
individuals, which is, after all, the heart of McPhee's work and the heart
of this frontier. As Ronald Weber points out, "In and around Eagle,
McPhee finds characters of sufficient interest to populate a dozen novels."[11] The question introduced in the opening of the book—"What is to
be the fate of this land?"—is transformed in the final section into "What
will be the fate of these individuals?" What, McPhee asks in the myriad
profiles in *Coming into the Country,* will be the fate of the pioneering spirit
that is an integral part of the American character?

   As Barbara Lounsberry has aptly pointed out, *Coming into the Country*
is one of McPhee's most Thoreauvian volumes. McPhee, as she says,
"goes to a cabin in the wilderness to confront the essential facts of
Alaska."[12] And similar to Thoreau, McPhee spent approximately two
years off and on at his Walden Pond. It is the bush that seems to truly
define what Alaska is and the people who have "come into the country"
that define the bush. Therefore, it is in Eastern Alaska, near the Yukon
Territory, principally around the small town of Eagle, that McPhee centers his search. There is a clannish sense of place among people in the
bush. Although they may have many points of disagreement, most of
them seem to agree about one thing—the significance of the wilderness.

   Donna Kneeland, recently come into the country, is the subject of
McPhee's initial look at the pioneer spirit. Like Carol Ruckdeschel,
Donna is a beautiful young woman, strong, knowledgeable, and determined. Unlike Carol, the twenty-eight-year-old Donna does not believe
it is prudent to live alone in the wild—but McPhee's description of her
independent character makes the reader believe that she would be able
to, and may one day outgrow her companion Dick Cook. Donna is a
rarity in Alaska—a white woman who was born there (in Juneau) and
who grew up in various locations around the state. A short stay in
Edmonton, Canada, left her with an undeniable yearning to live away
from civilization. So she did what any practical young woman might
do—she hunted for a suitable trapper to share her life with in the
wilderness. McPhee describes how she stalked the meetings of the Interior Alaska Trappers Association and came upon Dick Cook, who had
been in the country for the better part of a decade.

   Cook, who lives in a cabin near a tributary of the Yukon River fifty
miles into the wild from the town of Eagle, is a trapper by trade and, as
McPhee suggests, a "sachem figure" (192) by instinct. Like many of the
people in the New Jersey Pine Barrens, Cook is not afraid of work,
"claiming that to lower his income and raise his independence he has

worked twice as hard as most people" (186). One of Cook's main precepts is that he tries not to make more money than is absolutely necessary (188). Cook and Kneeland, like Rich Corazzo and so many others who came to the Alaskan bush, seek not "a living so much as a life" (272). In Cook, Kneeland found the ideal outdoorsman, part Davy Crockett and part Daniel Boone. He is all pragmatist; there is nothing of the romantic about him. He is skilled in the ways of surviving in the wilderness. McPhee catalogues Cook's skills: he traps, he hunts, he gardens. He travels by canoe or dog sled. If his tooth needs to be pulled, he wraps a pair of channel-lock pliers with tape and attempts the job himself. He has an uncanny sense of place. Although he uses several hundred trap lines he remembers where every one is "with no trouble" (188). Cook is reminiscent of Henri Vaillancourt in his skillfulness but in his arrogance and pedantry, as well. Sultan-like, he treats Donna and others as if they were his subordinates. No one is to sit in his chair; no one is to speak while he is talking. He has the sort of pridefulness that makes him seem like a good candidate to be a protagonist in a Flannery O'Connor short story. But he exists in the real world, and the world that he exists in is not for the weak. In Cook's vocabulary, the word *ecology* means "who's eating whom, and when" (417). Cook looks like "a scarecrow made of cables" (189); he is a survivor, essentially a lone wolf. Donna Kneeland is there with him, a follower with her guru, and even though she knows how to tan hides, plant crops, and do an assortment of other tasks, she will always be a lesser being in his Darwinian universe. Finally, though, McPhee leaves it to the reader to make any judgments about Cook, and like the people in town, the reader is left with contradictory views—"pontifical, messianic" or "a patient hunter . . . a wealth of information" (205).

There is an epic cast of characters in and around Eagle, the locus for McPhee's observations of Alaska's people and the center of the circle of his explorations into the bush. John Borg is a jack of all trades, "a one-man city" (193), the postmaster, president of the Eagle Historical Society, local reporter for the National Weather Service, and mayor. Mike Potts is expert in surviving in the mountains, as Dick Cook is in the river country. Michael David represents all that is positive and spiritual in the Indian village. People like Viola Goggins, who came into the country with "a baby and a dime, and only the baby had substantially grown" (206), and Jim Dungan, who lives comfortably in an eight-by-twelve-foot cabin—"not quite three steps by four" (218)—are typical of the subsistence living that many people accept to be away from the cities.

There is a Thoreauvian echo in the voices of many of these characters, a choral voice that McPhee uses to reflect the individuality and diversity of the Alaskan community. Brad Snow and Lilly Allen, for example, came to the Alaskan bush "to do without unnecessary things, to live out, to deal with the land in a more natural way" (241–2). McPhee brings many of these characters to life with epigrammatic, funny descriptions. Jim Scott has a "slicing edge in his demeanor, as if someone had just put a question to him concerning his expense account" (369). Harry David is "the kind of man who shakes Tabasco on his beans" (384), and Junior Biederman "looks like a Mexican insurrectionist ten years after the coup" (398). The handsome Lilly Allen is "facially Puritan, sober, with a touch of anachronism about her, as if on Sundays somehow she occupies a front pew, listening to Cotton Mather" (241).

The Pioneer Spirit and the Preservation of Place

If any group of people epitomizes the resilient, unpretentious pioneer spirit, the Gelvins do. Both Ed and Stanley Gelvin, father and son, are skilled in the ways of living in the country. They are men of "maximum practical application" (232), as one of McPhee's other characters says. Projects that would daunt most people, like dismantling a bulldozer and flying it piece by piece into a mountain location where they can reassemble it and use it to dig for gold, are for them like solving a difficult but manageable algebra problem. If there are any unequivocal heroes in *Coming into the Country* the Gelvins may be the ones. Capable, industrious, inventive, the Gelvins are a match for the land, for this place where "civilization stops" and only certain people are willing and able to go "deep into the roadless world" (246).

The Gelvins are gold miners, not members of the Sierra Club. They hunt wolves, and dig deep into the beautiful mountains. It is near the end of the book, after suggesting his respect for the magnificence of the Alaskan landscape that McPhee offers his surprising conclusions about the Gelvins's mining and their relationship to place:

> This mine is a cork on the sea. Meanwhile (and, possibly, more seriously), the relationship between father and son is as attractive as anything I have seen in Alaska—both of them self-reliant beyond the usual reach of the term, the characteristic formed by this country. Whatever they are doing, whether it is mining or something else, they do for themselves what no one else is here to do for them. Their kind is more endangered

every year. Balance that against the nick they are making in the land. Only an easygoing extremist would preserve every bit of the country. And extremists would exploit it all. Everyone else has to think the matter through—choose a point of tolerance, however much the point might tend to one side. For myself, I am closer to the preserving side—that is, the side that would preserve the Gelvins. To be sure, I would preserve plenty of land as well. (430)

The Gelvins fit into their environment as smoothly as the Eskimos do or the crofters on Colonsay. The life in Alaska that attracts the Gelvins and people like them has "great liabilities and . . . great possibilities" (229). It is a place for people like Jack Boone who are not impressed with "the advantages of modern civilization" (337). People like the Gelvins, as Joe Vogler, another resident of the country, says, "would be misfits somewhere else. They're doers. They don't destroy. They build. They preserve" (317).

As in *The Pine Barrens* and *Encounters with the Archdruid*, in *Coming into the Country* McPhee presents no simple resolution to the conflicts. He offers no easy answers, but he does clearly admire the Thoreauvian spirit in many of the residents of Eagle and Circle, Alaska. In his admiration for them and his love of the land, he seems to call for a balance, a preservation of both the environment and the American character. The tough spirit and the ruggedly beautiful landscape are inextricably linked.

In the final image of *Coming into the Country*, McPhee describes his meeting with a young man who has just come into the country, stocked up with supplies in Eagle General Stores, and is off into the woods. The reader is left to decide whether the newcomer has what it will take to survive in the bush. McPhee shapes the conclusion in this way: "I asked him where he meant to go. 'Down the river,' he said. 'I'll be living on the Yukon and getting my skills together.' I wished him heartfelt luck and felt in my heart he would need it. I said my name, and shook his hand, and he said his. He said, 'My name is River Wind' " (*Country*, 438).

It may be doubtful that this immense young man in a wide-brimmed black hat will make it in the country. The winter after McPhee meets him, no one in the town remembers River Wind. He is just one of the dozens who tries his luck in the wilderness, but he is one more example of the need for this frontier. It is there for people to re-imagine their lives, for individuals with an adventurous instinct to seek a new life.

McPhee suggests throughout *Coming into the Country* and a number of his other books that if the wilderness is tamed, developed, covered in asphalt and shopping malls, then something wild and necessary in the spirit of human beings will also be lost. For McPhee a sense of place is not just the prerequisite for the good basketball player or the ship's captain—it is a vital part of what it means to be human, a wanderer's sense of the meaning of *home*.

Chapter Six
Science and Technology

The word *science* derives from the Latin for *knowledge*. The universe that McPhee seeks out and the one that he writes about is filled with men and women of experience and action, but it is populated by individuals, like scientists and technicians, who cherish the forms of knowledge that will enable them to create and invent. Most often, McPhee's scientists are men and women who look for ways of applying theory to their everyday worlds. The word *technology,* which stems from the Greek for the study of an art or craft, may be the ideal subject for a man like McPhee who is fascinated by skill in its various forms and shapes.

McPhee understands that science and technology are linked inextricably to one another, and that technology, which has been part of the history of humankind since the discovery of stone implements and the control of fire, is a mixed blessing. Modern technology has brought the world out of the darkness, but the light it sheds is not always pleasant. Technology develops faster than most people are able to follow. Therefore, it is often difficult to measure the consequences of innovation. Technology has left us with the potential of nuclear power but its apocalyptic dangers as well.

The Curve of Binding Energy

In *The Curve of Binding Energy,* published in 1974, McPhee tells the story of a scientist, Theodore B. Taylor, and the dangerous possibilities inherent in the most powerful technologies that humans have thus far invented. McPhee is often at his best elucidating complex information, and in *The Curve of Binding Energy* he works with some of his most complicated material. John Skow in *Time* magazine said, "Writing about nuclear physics and the creative process of a bomb maker for an audience that does not understand mathematics, moreover, is a bit like writing music criticism for the deaf. McPhee manages very well, using the life and thought of Theoretical Physicist Ted Taylor as a way into the subject. The reader, balancing his head carefully so that the neutrons won't spill out, is led an enormous distance, to the point where a good many of Taylor's calculations seem understandable."[1]

What seems most understandable and most dramatically rendered in the book is the awesome danger in the technology of atomic power and the sometimes mind-boggling ineptitude in the industry that has grown up around uranium and plutonium. In *The Curve of Binding Energy* McPhee glides back and forth between his profile of Taylor, a central figure in the creation of efficient atomic bombs, and the burgeoning of the industry itself. As Sandra Schmidt Oddo said, McPhee is like a documentary film maker: "Give him a theme and he comes up with a picture: edited, cross-cut, spliced and orchestrated, specific and full of the facts and the atmosphere of that theme. The picture, like a good documentary, carries its own emotional impact as well as, in this case, an urgent imperative."[2] The theme and the emotional imperative are embodied in Ted Taylor. Barbara Lounsberry feels that Taylor is the "quintessential American hero" and a character that resembles McPhee's the most in the writer's canon because Taylor "represents a virtuoso performance up and down the periodic table and across the levels of the atomic sphere."[3]

As Lounsberry would suggest, Taylor, like McPhee, is a genius of circles and spheres. Surely, Taylor is a genius, especially if one defines the term as the novelist Steven Millhauser did in *Edwin Mullhouse* as the childlike "retention of the capacity to be obsessed."[4] Throughout his career Taylor had the knack of blocking out the world around him as he pondered larger or smaller circles. He would forget time and the rainfall on the roof of his rustic cabin as he explained to McPhee how an atomic bomb could readily be made. On his way to lunch he would ride past his favorite Chinese restaurant, missing it as he thought of ways to separate uranium and plutonium oxides. Thinking of other worlds, he would repeatedly try to start his car with a hotel key. He was a stargazer, a man who dreamed of going to Mars and Pluto in a rocket he designed that would be powered by atomic bombs. In a sense, his portrait fits the shape of the well-known absent-minded genius: "Sometimes at the family dinner table, Ted Taylor will leave a conversation. He simply goes away, in every sense but the physical presence of his body in a chair. He stays away for varying lengths of time. When his thoughts have made their journey and come back, he will resume a conversation at the exact place he left it, as if all animation in the world had been suspended while he was gone" (*Curve*, 165).

But Taylor, as McPhee suggests, is an original. He flunked out of his doctoral program at the University of California at Berkeley, failing his oral preliminary exams twice as he haltingly attempted to explain the

Second Law of Thermodynamics to three senior professors. Like a long line of geniuses before him, from Copernicus to Faulkner, he had followed his own interests—"I like to do what I like to do" (59). Clearly, he was an exceptional student, graduating from high school at fifteen and from college at nineteen, but his brilliance was of a special sort. When he went to Exeter for an additional year of secondary education, he barely noticed that he received a D in modern physics because he was so fascinated by the "submicroscopic solar systems" (29) that he was peering into for the first time. Taylor, as one of his professors at Berkeley realized, was not a typical scholar or analyst, but rather, as McPhee says, "He was a conceiver of things" (59).

McPhee shows Taylor's uniqueness through the eyes of those who know him. Others soon saw Taylor's uniqueness. The scientist Freeman Dyson understood that Taylor was not a brilliant mathematician or physicist. Instead he was, as Dyson remembers him,

> a special kind of physicist, with a feeling for something as a concrete object rather than for equations you write down about it. In a European system, after an experience such as the one he had at Berkeley, he would never have had a chance. I have a low opinion of higher education. Ted had no time for such nonsense, and in this respect he was like Einstein. He was like Einstein, too, in his style of thinking. Both were theoretical. Neither did physics experiments in the conventional sense. Both of them were extraordinarily unmathematical. Ted thinks of real things. (172–3)

As Dyson saw him, Taylor was a Columbus without an America to discover, but a Columbus, nevertheless, and "perhaps the greatest man that I ever knew well" (173). As Stanislaw Ulam, the co-inventor of the hydrogen bomb, saw Taylor, he was a Jules Verne American. Ulam says, "When I met Ted, he fitted the ideas I formed as a boy of Americans, as represented by Jules Verne. The trait I noticed immediately was inventiveness. . . . He was intense, high-strung, introspective. 'If something is possible, let's do it' was Ted's attitude" (120). Taylor grew up in Mexico City in the 1930s when the spirit of revolution was still in the air and every politician seemed to carry a pearl-handled Colt .45. Growing up, Ted did seem like a character in a Jules Verne novel, dreaming of big white discs. He had recurrent dreams of planets, "discs filling his field of vision, filling all his nerves with terror" (12). He experimented with a chemistry set he had been given for Christmas, making guncotton and other small explosives. As McPhee describes him, he began to learn his physics by playing billiards nearly every day after school, understanding "empirically the behavior of the interacting balls on the table, all within the confining framework of the reflector cushions" (10).

McPhee explains that Taylor outgrew the chemistry lab and billiard balls and began to contemplate the smallest and largest of circles, atoms and planets. As a bomb designer at Los Alamos in his twenties and thirties, he conceived Davy Crockett, the lightest and smallest fission bomb ever made up to that point. He also designed Hamlet, the most efficient fission bomb ever made in the kiloton range, and the Super Oralloy Bomb, the largest-yield fission bomb that had ever been exploded. In 1956 Taylor left Los Alamos so that he could focus his attention on the peaceful use of atoms for space exploration in a project called Orion. He envisioned nuclear energy, the power of two thousand atomic bombs powering a rocket, opening up the universe to human beings for new frontiers. As Freeman Dyson said, "It was . . . something more than looking through the keyhole of the universe. It was opening the door wide" (184). Taylor saw Project Orion as a way of guaranteeing the survival of the planet. McPhee explains Taylor's reasoning this way:

> After running through the resources on its own planet, a given civilization would then logically turn to the nearest sun. The minuscule fraction of total sunlight that actually strikes a planet could not be of extensive use, so a resource-impoverished civilization, in order to assure almost indefinite survival, would send giant plates of materials into orbit around its sun, forming a great discontinuous shell, a titanic nonrigid sphere, conserving almost all the heat and light and photosynthetic sustenance the sun would give. (171–2)

Taylor and his fellow scientists imagined dismantling a neighboring planet and using the materials as a shell around the sun. This sounds like the plot of a Jules Verne story, but for Taylor it was realistic and feasible, and perhaps there is more McPhee than Verne in all of this—a parable of individuality and engagement with the world. The limited-test-ban treaty of 1963, however, stopped all nuclear explosions in space and, ironically, put a stop to Project Orion and a potentially peaceful use of nuclear power.

Taylor came to regret his involvement in designing bombs and feared that atomic weapons would be used by terrorists and criminals. The change in attitude from bomb maker to advocate of strong regulations of the nuclear industry was not a hundred eighty degree shift for Taylor. It was more of a circling back to his original position. As a teenage midshipman going to school at Throgs Neck in the Bronx, Taylor wrote a letter home after he heard of the destruction of Hiroshima by the atomic bomb:

> My first reaction to the news was one of almost horror, in spite of the fact that I think the end of the war is a matter of weeks . . . my fear is that man has discovered something which, knowing so very little about it, may destroy him. The discovery will undoubtedly be common knowledge to all the governments of the world before long. Therefore, it seems to me that this must either be the last war or the nations of the world will completely destroy each other. And it will only be through radical changes in the world's economic, social, and political systems that a complete catastrophe can be prevented. . . . The atom bomb and what it represents can easily be the means to end all wars. (33)

Early in his career at Los Alamos, Taylor at times seemed able, like the character of Felix Hoenniker in Kurt Vonnegut's *Cat's Cradle,* to view a bomb test without focusing on the moral consequences. McPhee writes, "He [Taylor] spent what he remembers as 'essentially no time' contemplating that Scorpion might be reproduced as a weapon for killing human beings. He marvelled instead at the exceptional clarity of the Nevada air and how the distances he could see were so great they were deceiving" (93). At some level during his work at Los Alamos, Taylor was firmly convinced of the deterrent possibilities of nuclear weapons, but by the time he left New Mexico, his belief in bombs as deterrent had "eroded to zero."

> I thought I was doing my part for my country. I thought I was contributing to a permanent state of peace. I no longer feel that way. I wish I hadn't done it. The whole thing was wrong. Rationalize how you will, the bombs were designed to kill many, many people. I sometimes can't blame people if they wish all scientists were lined up and shot. If it were possible to wave a wand and make fission impossible—fission of any kind—I would quickly wave the wand. I have a total conviction—now—that nuclear weapons should not be used under any circumstances. At any time. Anywhere. Period. If I were king. If the Russians bombed New York. I would not bomb Moscow. (120–1)

But, as McPhee makes clear, fission does exist and Taylor is not king; therefore, in 1967 he formed a firm called International Research & Technology to serve as a private monitor of nuclear-materials safeguards and to assist in preventing individuals, groups, or nations from misappropriating fissile material and making a bomb.

In essence, *The Curve of Binding Energy,* a book about bombs and bomb makers, is actually, as Barbara Lounsberry suggests, a "rhetorical bomb" itself, out to explode some myths and wake the public up to the real and immediate dangers surrounding them.[5] The book begins with a dark warning that Taylor, an expert in the field, is certain that it is possible for an individual or group to make an atomic bomb, and as the nuclear industry proliferates, the necessary materials will only become more accessible. With Taylor, McPhee travels to nuclear power plants where heavy-lidded guards barely notice unmarked pickup trucks zipping in and out of the compound, where flimsy chain-link fences and unsophisticated alarms are feeble deterrents, where uranium and plutonium could be plucked, it seems, by a reasonably organized college fraternity during hell week.

As Joan Hamilton points out in an essay in *Sierra,* McPhee immersed himself in his subject. Hamilton spoke with Ted Taylor, who said that McPhee would work from six in the morning until nine-thirty at night when the two traveled together in the early 1970s. According to Taylor, McPhee always had an open notebook and a sharpened pencil. "Taylor would brief him in the morning, and then they'd tour a nuclear facility. At each stage, as he moved from room to room talking with plant personnel, 'he would not proceed until he understood what was happening,' Taylor says. 'I had enormous admiration for his capacity to stay intellectually alert.' "[6]

The Curve of Binding Energy is a portrait of genius, but it is also a portrait of the potentially terrible consequences of genius. As always, McPhee is fascinated by craftsmen, by makers, by technocrats who change the world. McPhee is interested in explaining the intricacies of craft, of science. Often, he is able to explain technical matters with such liveliness and clarity that scientists are amazed at his ability to transform their thoughts into such supple prose. In *The Curve of Binding Energy* he chose a subject that has life-and-death consequences, and this makes his pellucid descriptions seem to resonate with a strange sort of power:

Fuel rods are chopped up, like stalks of celery under a kitchen knife, by a mighty guillotine that cleanly severs steel. Now all the small cuttings are dissolved in nitric acid, and the resulting radioactive fluid begins to travel up and down through a series of tanks and tubes, arranged in tall columnar form, where the addition of reactive chemicals—tributyl, phosphate, dodecane—effects the separation of plutonium and unconsumed uranium not only from each other but also from a variety of radioactive fission products, such as strontium-90, krypton-85, and cesium-137. At the far end of the canyon, uranium hexafluoride comes out through a hole in the wall. Plutonium-nitrate solution pours from a nearby spigot. (39)

There is something eerie in this scene, uranium seeping from a hole and plutonium pouring from a spigot. The clarity of McPhee's descriptions and reporting give the whole story a surreal quality at times, but straightforward prose underscores the point that Taylor (and McPhee) wish to make—that it might not be that difficult to understand this process of the power of binding energy and to recreate the technology that unleashes "the strength of the forces that bind the parts of the atomic nucleus together" (160). Taylor's plaintive cry is direct: "a deadline is on us; it is almost too late" (227). McPhee's judgment is a bit more laced with irony and sarcasm, but it echoes Taylor's sentiment: " 'Every civilization must go through this,' Taylor repeats. 'Those that don't make it destroy themselves. Those that do make it wind up cavorting all over the universe.' As I followed him around the country, people kept asking me, more often than I can count from memory, if I realized the size of the investment that is already implanted in the nuclear industry and how damaging to that investment any major change in the industry's patterns could be. I concluded that other civilizations may have died rich" (232).

"The Atlantic Generating Station"

A few years after the publication of *The Curve of Binding Energy,* in "The Atlantic Generating Station" (included in the collection *Giving Good Weight*), McPhee once again turns his attention to man's most powerful technology, nuclear power. In this story, McPhee reports on a rather strange plan to construct huge nuclear power plants, mounted on gigantic hulls, that will float upon the ocean. They would be traveling plants, moving from one part of the ocean to another. As odd as the idea sounds, McPhee explains that there were some precedents—ships used as power plants during World War II and submarines that now use nuclear reactors.

The idea for the floating nuclear plants was first conceived by Richard Eckert, a New Jersey Public Service and Gas Company engineer, as he took a shower one morning before work. It is Eckert's job to find appropriate sites for new power plants in the state, but in New Jersey, the most densely populated of the fifty, it was not an easy task to find a suitable place to locate a new plant. A power plant needed space, and it needed plenty of water to cool it—"five hundred acres of ground and a million gallons a minute" (*Giving*, 78).

Richard Eckert is a common type of McPhee character—a visionary but also an ordinary man. Like Bradley or Gibbons or the makers of the Aereon 26 in *The Deltoid Pumpkin Seed*, Eckert sees what others cannot readily see. Like Ted Taylor's family, Eckert's sees him as a slightly bemused genius. When Eckert tells his wife, for instance, about his plan to launch power plants like ships in the ocean, her response is—"There you go again" (79). On the surface he appears to be a typical individual—slightly balding; accustomed to his daily commute to Newark; prone to wearing gray suits, gray socks, black shoes, and white shirts; apt to be found on the weekends sailing the New Jersey inlets with his children. But to many along the New Jersey coast, after his vision of floating nuclear plants, he became, according to McPhee, the "Antichrist" (80).

Eckert's plan was for the construction of the offshore breakwater to begin in 1981, for the first station to be floating in 1985, and for the second to be riding the waves by 1987. In a postscript, McPhee makes it clear that the floating power plants are "an idea whose time had not yet come" (118). And the plants seemed even less likely to be built in the wake of Three Mile Island, "the nuclear plant on the Susquehanna that in the early spring of 1979 seemed to be preparing to relocate itself on the banks of the Yangtze River" (118). There seems to be no particular edge in McPhee's voice, no specific glee or sense of sadness, when he announces that the plants will not be built in the near future. He appears to take neither side in the debate, as if he senses some of the absurdity and, perhaps, danger in the situation and at the same time admires the quixotic visions of technical experts like Eckert. McPhee reports and leaves it to the reader to form an opinion about what the future will or should hold. "Like bulbs around a mirror, floating nuclear plants might one day edge the seas. People who thought the concept was madness still had much time in which to say so. People who thought the concept was among the best of possible alternatives could present their case as well. More than fifty construction and operating permits were absolutely required. So far, not one had been issued" (118).

During the course of the story, with a carefully maintained balance, McPhee explains the ideas of the technicians like Eckert, but he also discusses the possible effects of such power plants on ocean life, the consequences that could come from a rapid shift in water temperature, the effect on moon snails, flounder, sand shrimp, spotted hake. In addition, he speculates about how the ocean life could affect such nuclear plants. "Summer trawls had yielded, typically, sea robins, dogfish and other sharks, scup, perch, menhaden. Menhaden were the most numerous fish of the region. A school of them might weigh sixteen tons. Sixteen tons of menhaden could be a problem against the screens. A massive impingement of menhaden could shut the plant down" (101).

He describes what will have to occur before such plants could be set into operation—dredging and grading the ocean floor, concrete caissons sunk to the bottom, a hill of rock built sixty-four feet into the air above the waves. It seems a grand, dangerous project, an act of technology that would point to what is most vital, imaginative, unconquerable in the human spirit. Or it could suggest a dangerous use of science, man's dreams possibly turning to nightmares, technology, like Karel Capek's robots, with the potential to turn on its creators. McPhee, like a novelist, tells his story, leaving it up to the reader to decide if there are any clear villains or fools in the tale.

"Minihydro"

In "Minihydro," which was included in the collection *Table of Contents,* McPhee offers a less equivocal, clearly more admiring look at technological innovators. "Minihydro" is the story of entrepreneurs who, in the aftermath of the National Energy Act of 1978 in which Congress made it profitable for small-scale hydroelectric facilities to sell power to the territorial utilities, search for "places where the power of falling water had for one purpose or another been utilized in the past" (*Table,* 204). The Energy Act declared that anyone who made power at a small-scale hydroelectric facility could sell the power for absorption into the regional grid for an amount that would match the rising price of oil. This meant a "modern bonanza" (205) in minihydros. The rush for riches reminds McPhee a bit of the gold rush in the Yukon at the end of the nineteenth century, except these prospectors are looking for weirs, abandoned power sheds, sluiceways, and old turbines.

McPhee follows the trails of a few private power pioneers, men and women who resemble people like the Gelvins in *Coming into the Country.* Whether these minihydro entrepreneurs are retired owners of resin plants, aspiring writers of fiction, potters, or even an undergraduate at the University of Massachusetts, majoring in finance, who joins forces with his professor to start his own company, the individuals that McPhee describes are self-reliant, capable of breathing life into their

dreams. McPhee suggests that this is technology used for a double good.
These innovators, searching into the past to make use of it in the present, finding small privately owned hydroelectric plants that have been
abandoned, save fossil fuels without creating more waste. This technology also gives shape and direction to the practical creative spirit that
McPhee writes of with such respect and admiration.

The Deltoid Pumpkin Seed

One of McPhee's most delightful and eccentric descriptions of technology appears in *The Deltoid Pumpkin Seed,* published in 1973. It is the
story of another collection of dreamers, technological pioneers who are,
in a sense, going forward and backward at the same time. The book may
be an example of what McPhee does best—in terms of the originality of
the characters, the clarity of the technical descriptions, and the power of
the idiosyncratic story of ordinary people caught up in an adventure that
tests their talents, imagination, and perseverance.

In an interview, McPhee discussed the merits of the book. "Nonfiction writers go out not knowing what to expect. In a way you're like a
cook foraging for materials, and in many ways, like a cook, you're only
as good as your materials. You go out looking for characters to sketch,
arresting places to describe, dialogue to capture—the way you would
gather berries. You hope for the greatest variety. Perhaps the work that
best exemplifies what I'm talking about, this sort of variety, is *The Deltoid Pumpkin Seed.* I'm not saying it's the 'best,' but it is a good example
of what I reach for in my writing."[7] *The Deltoid Pumpkin Seed* is an eclectic blend of technical description, characterization, and the study of
organizational politics. It is both comedy and drama, simultaneously
laced with suspense and punctuated by slapstick. It is the story of the
dream of a completely new airship, not an airplane and not exactly a
dirigible but an "aerobody," as William Miller, the president of Aereon
Corporation, constantly reminds those around him. It is the story of the
machine and of the half dozen men who influence its shape and direction. It is the story of zeppelins, the Hindenburg, and improbable
dreams in general.

Aereon Corporation started as an idea that sprung into the head of
Monroe Drew in the late 1950s. McPhee, a writer who seems to relish
digressions and odd connections, spends a good amount of time detailing Drew's unusual history. He was the pastor at the Fourth Presbyte-
rian Church in Trenton, New Jersey, and a chaplain at the Naval Reserve

Training Center. He was not a pilot, but he knew enough about dirigibles to explain the concept to his young son who came home from elementary school one day with a question about them. He was the author and originator of Teleprayer in Trenton and the maker of a few religious films during his eight years of active duty as a chaplain in the Navy—not exactly obvious qualifications to become the designer of a new type of aircraft—but he began to sketch lighter-than-air vehicles that could carry enormous loads. His idea was that the aircraft could carry Bibles and food to needy countries. His sketches became a serious interest and eventually an obsession. Drew met John Fitzpatrick, a lieutenant commander in the Navy and an expert in lighter-than-air craft, and the two formed Aereon Corporation in 1959. Drew felt that Fitzpatrick was a "godsend"—a man who could "design and build Drew's dreams" (38).

But Drew and Fitzpatrick are minor characters in McPhee's saga of aerobodies. The central character may be William Miller, the president of the company when McPhee writes his story. Miller came to the company a few years after Drew began the organization. Coincidentally, Miller is also a minister. He had just received his degree of Master of Theology from Princeton Theological Seminary, and he was wondering what kind of church work to do and, as well, what to do with his sizable inheritance. Like some of McPhee's other characters, Miller is brilliant but not necessarily understood by those around him. He had just been denied entry into the Th.D. program at Princeton and had the terminal master's placed in his hand. This, along with the fact that he was an ex-Navy jet fighter pilot, may have led him to notice something in his financial broker's office. As McPhee says, "He literally did not know what to do with his money or with himself. His glance fell on a picture that was on a broker's desk—a romantic sketch, photographically reproduced, of a triple-hulled dirigible soaring into a mottled, darkling sky. On the side of the dirigible was the word 'Aereon'" (120). By 1970 Miller had invested the better part of a decade and "something like three hundred thousand dollars of his own money into Aereon, almost totally evaporating his inheritance, his portfolio, and even his Navy flight pay, every cent of which he had saved" (14). He had taken over the company from Drew, who had become "founder non grata" (136), and Miller, who had the "capacity to be a passionate believer" (134) and believed in Aereon fervently. It became for him a religious conviction. His obsession is both his singularity and his oddity.

McPhee, wondering about Miller's motives, ponders his deeper purposes: "Personal profit could hardly be the radical motivation of a man who had poured away three hundred thousand dollars without apparent qualm. Monklike, frugal, denying himself every sweet in the box, he had spent (by then) several years singlemindedly struggling to preserve this checkered company" (137). Although Miller had always wanted to be an Aereonautical engineer, he "felt inexorably drawn to a higher calling" (142). Aviation and religion seemed a logical combination, a passionate belief in one, perhaps, helping to sustain a belief in the other.

Subjects to write about come to McPhee in a variety of ways. Many subjects, as he has said, come from interests he had as a young man at Camp Keewaydin in Vermont. Others come through happenstance, meeting an art smuggler on Amtrak or following the scent of oranges from Grand Central Station in New York to the groves of Florida. Some come from friends or acquaintances who whisper in his ear about unusual characters or strange adventures. But the story that became *The Deltoid Pumpkin Seed*, like the tale that became *The Pine Barrens*, was close to home. Miller graduated from Princeton in 1953, the same year that McPhee did. And Miller's offices for Aereon Corporation were in rooms above a bank on Nassau Street in Princeton, not far from the same bank that housed McPhee's office for a number of years and where he wrote *Coming into the Country* and a number of other books, including *The Deltoid Pumpkin Seed*.

The Deltoid Pumpkin Seed was close to home in a deeper sense, too. Miller, like other McPhee heroes, has the capacity to be obsessed, but the book has other men of singular vision and talent. There is a gallery of McPhee heroes. John Olcott is a test pilot who has the steely nerves and steady-handed calm that people associate with the breed. The only time he shows any fear occurs when he realizes that he forgot to put gas in his car, something he often forgets to do. But the thirty-five-year-old Olcott "hardly appeared to be the sort of creature who dances around on the lips of danger seeking the pleasures of not being swallowed" (11). He looks more like "the president of anybody's student council some years ago" (11). William Putman is an aerodynamicist who believes in the "aesthetics of function" (74), a phrase that could describe many of McPhee's practical artists. Everett Linkenhoker, John Weber, and Charlie Mills are all individuals whose talents move them in the direction of creating something vital.

John Kukon, though, may be one of the most strangely appealing of McPhee's characters. Kukon works at Princeton University as a professional model maker. Like Ted Taylor, Kukon is precocious, as a high school student making Class A models, proto-speeds, and jets, winning races in all classes. He set two national records in one week and won three hundred fifty trophies in his career. He started building gasoline-powered flying model airplanes when he was seven years old. Like Henri Vaillancourt without some of the self-absorption, Kukon never wanted to fly, just to make models. His whole life seemed to be devoted to making models, and although it is hard to imagine that there is a place in the world for such a man, with such a talent, there was. In explaining how Kukon found his profession, McPhee seems delighted and a bit surprised himself: "After high school, he had enrolled at the Academy of Aereonautics at La Guardia Airport, where he got his Airframe and Powerplant credentials, the badge of the licensed mechanic. He had been about to go to work at Newark Airport as a mechanic for American Airlines when a friend told him about a job at Princeton that seemed unbelievable. The university actually paid people to build models" (25). Kukon went to work at the test facility called Long Track, where they tested models of low-speed craft. There he became "a master builder of aircraft models with a virtuosity few other people had ever approached" (18). It is Kukon's twenty-inch Aereon, made of balsa wood and tissue paper, with a rubber band for a motor, that gives the company its first flight.

Kukon and the others involved in the corporation watch the gradual rise of Aereon, the deltoid pumpkin seed, painted a Princeton orange, somehow preposterous and magnificent, until they see it soar in the final test. With John Olcott piloting the airship, it climbs to five hundred feet and floats along at sixty-four knots with the skyline of Atlantic City as a backdrop and past the wide marshes and the bays. Their dream, in part, like the dreams of Henri Vaillancourt or the entrepreneurs in "Minihydro," is a recapitulation of the past, a circling back to Solomon Andrews, another New Jersey native, who, in the mid-nineteenth century, designed and flew the first dirigible, years before Count Zeppelin put a rigid airship into the skies. Andrews was a Renaissance man— physician, inventor, mayor of Perth Amboy—but he was a man, like Miller or Drew, who considered the Aereons to be "the purpose of his life, his real destiny" (125).

McPhee explains that Andrews's dirigible, powered by gravity, was made up of three cylinders each eighty feet long, sewn together and covered with varnished linen. The 8 September 1863, issue of the New York *Herald* called Andrews's accomplishment "the most extraordinary invention of the age, if not the most so of any the world ever saw—at least the greatest stride in invention ever made by a single individual"

(97). Andrews saw his invention as a gigantic lemon seed, and he published a pamphlet titled "The Art of Flying: Without Eccentricity There is No Progress" (100). But despite Andrews's initial success, his experience with dirigibles seems have to foreshadowed the experiences of the twentieth-century Aereon Corporation. Andrews's idea found a receptive audience in the War Department during the Civil War, but once the war ended and the president was assassinated, everyone seemed to forget about his airship. When a depression struck the economy, he ran out of money and funding, and he died a few years later, leaving himself behind as a footnote in *A History of the Medical Society of New Jersey* as the creator of the "world's first dirigible" (104–5).

But, as McPhee explains in his summary of the history of rigid airships, which he places in the center of his narrative about Aereon past and present, it was the most famous of dirigibles—the Hindenburg—that most likely dealt the death blow to them in the public consciousness. Ironically, it was in Lakehurst, New Jersey, in 1937, that the Hindenburg burned while moored there. The people of New Jersey seem to have a strange attraction to the dirigibles, what McPhee calls "these phallic, Wagnerian rigids, brushed with mist" (115). Therefore, it may be understandable that the "billowing holocaustal white fire" (115) burned deep into their collective imagination and the thirty-four-second blaze left nothing but ash, soft aluminum, and tragic associations from then on for such aircraft. "The Graf Zeppelin, on the way home from Rio de Janeiro, was approaching the Canary Islands at the time. The radio operator picked up the news, and the captain decided not to inform the passengers. Their voyage was the last voyage of the rigid airships. . . . All schedules were cancelled. The ships were, before long, disassembled. At the height of their development, the height of their performance, the rigid airships disappeared" (116). But, as *The Deltoid Pumpkin Seed* dramatizes, the dream of dirigible travel, as farfetched as the lemon seed or pumpkin seed images are, will not disappear—any more than the dreamers of such technological visions will allow derisive laughter or failures or lack of financial support to crush their hopes.

McPhee concludes *The Deltoid Pumpkin Seed* with a technique reminiscent of a nineteenth-century novelist, an epilogue of sorts in which he gives the details of the main characters' lives after the principal events of the story. Monroe Drew is now designing the Aereon 500, a solar-powered ship, run by hot air produced by a parabolic mirror. John Kukon is still building models, at home and at Princeton University, as a vocation and an avocation. Others, like John Weber, Bill Putnam, and John

Olcott, have moved on to other ventures. The circle of dirigible experimenters was shrinking as it had in the nineteenth century and again in the middle of the twentieth century.[8] Only William Miller continues to work full time for Aereon Corporation. He still leads his Bible groups, lives in his garden apartment, and believes religiously in his dream. As McPhee says, "The summary results of all tests, all flights, all briefings and debriefings, all computations, two configurations, three propellers, one founder, four presidents, twelve years, nearly one and a half million expended dollars, and a hundred miles of circuit flight had been reduced to data that could be expressed on a single sheet of paper. Miller travelled around the country holding up data like a lamp" (184).

In McPhee's work, technology is neither good nor evil. It is a creation of humankind and as such can be used in a variety of ways—to heat and light our homes or to destroy our cities. The men and women who invent new machines can appear quixotic or visionary. Not all dreamers are visionaries and not all dreams soar: Some are orange pumpkin seeds that rise a mere twenty-four inches off the ground on the first attempt. But sometimes a preposterous idea, a wingless vehicle, perhaps, takes flight, and even though its ascent is "like driving a station wagon stuffed with cordwood up the side of a mountain in first gear" (168), it succeeds because of the stubborn belief and the inventive talents of some ordinary individuals.

McPhee is a writer who is fascinated by the workings of machines and the world. He is a writer who seems to relish the challenge of explaining the complexities of science and technology. If the etymology of the word *technology* suggests a study of intricate skills and those who possess them, it would be difficult to imagine a more skillful or better equipped writer to tell such stories.

Chapter Seven

Nature

It might be fair to say that John McPhee is a nature writer *malgre lui*. He has said, "I've written about nature and it is terribly important to me," but he bristles at being defined simply as a nature writer (Personal Interview). It is easy enough to see his point; he is a sports writer, a cultural reporter, a travel journalist, a science writer. Although not all nature writers are environmentalists, it is as if he senses that the term "nature writer" can often be aligned with the word "polemist." McPhee's style and intentions in his writing are closer to the novelist than they are to the editorialist. His first priority is not to write about issues but about people. Often they are people, like David Brower, the former director of the Sierra Club, or Dick Cook, the Alaskan pioneer, who have strong opinions about the natural world and human beings' place in it. McPhee's goal, however, is to allow the issues to come to life through the individual drama. The rib of theory stays securely attached to the human subjects he observes. He lets his characters speak for themselves and allows his readers the narrative space to draw their own inferences. Nevertheless, the majority of McPhee's books focus on nature, on the most serious questions that face us regarding preservation versus development, on the delicate balance between human expectation and responsibility in the natural world. Many of his stories are centered in wilderness areas, and quite a few of his profiles recount the lives of naturalists, environmentalists, and rural dwellers.

"The Keel of Lake Dickey"

"The Keel of Lake Dickey," which McPhee published in 1976, is an example of what is best in his nature writing and at the same time a departure from his typical methods. In the story, which was included in the collection *Giving Good Weight,* McPhee recounts a trip he took (four canoes and eight men) down the St. John River, a wide, majestic river that flows north from Maine into Canada. It is a big river, reminiscent of the Hudson in places, but it is a wild river, "the only Maine river of any size that has not been dammed" (*Giving,* 146). It goes free for two hundred miles until it reaches Canada, where "it has been both dammed and, in places, polluted on its way through New Brunswick to the sea" (146).

The purpose of McPhee's canoe trip through the north woods of Maine, similar to the one he took with John Kauffmann in Alaska (Kauffmann is also on this journey) and the one he took down the Colorado River with David Brower and Floyd Dominy, is to see the wild river before it is tamed for the purposes of civilization—a source of energy and recreation. The natural river is threatened by the oil crisis and America's desperate yearning for new sources of power. The vote by Congress to decide on appropriations for the construction funds to build the Dickey Dam, a means of generating new hydroelectric power and forming another recreation lake in Maine (a state that, as McPhee wryly points out, has two thousand lakes already), is in the offing.

During his river journey, McPhee suggests the importance of wilderness areas and the natural world to him. Nature soothes; it brings him back to himself. "Last night, I slept nine hours, rain thunking on the tent. Each night out here has been much the same. At home, I am lucky if I get five. Preoccupations there chase each other around, the strong ones fighting for the lead; and at three-thirty or four I get up and read, preferring the single track in a book to the whirling dozens in the brain. It's a chronic—or, at least, consistent—annoyance, and nights almost without exception are the same for me until I come to the woods, stretch out on the ground, and sleep nine hours" (137–8). The woods bring calm and permit sleep. A pilgrimage in the natural world forces attention to the elemental issues—"thoughts of weather, of food, and of the day's journey so dominate the mind that everything else subsides" (138–9).

While McPhee acknowledges the beauty and balm to be found in the natural world, he also recognizes the pain and annoyances to be discovered in the wild—the white-water canoeists who take their lives into their hands and dump in the frigid water or the black flies and no-see-ums "that mass on the skin and eat it as if they were acid" (158). If anything, McPhee is a stern-eyed Romantic with a sturdy sense of humor. Typically, it is balance he seeks, stylistically and thematically. He is rarely an extremist in his ideas about conserving nature or in his criticisms of technology. He worries about the effect of mining on the wilderness areas, but he makes it clear that the nick that people like the Gelvins make on the natural world should be "balanced" against the importance of preserving such a pioneer spirit. He is concerned about the proliferation of nuclear materials, but he views the possibilities of nuclear power with an open mind. Clearly, he cherishes nature and sees preserving the wilderness as a means of retaining a necessary wildness in the character of human beings. But ordinarily McPhee writes subtle parables about nature that compel his readers to think deeply about various sides of a question.

In "The Keel of Lake Dickey," McPhee alters this tactic slightly. What Joan Hamilton calls his rhetorical stance of "staunch openness" becomes more barbed. As Hamilton points out,

> Conclusions are indeed rare in McPhee's work, and where they do occur the author seems embarrassed by them. "I was screaming like Rumpelstiltskin in 'The Keel of Lake Dickey'. . . . A well-written editorial is a good thing—but it's not what I'm out to do." Instead McPhee aims to paint a scene so vivid that readers can experience it on their own terms, and walk away with their own well-informed opinions. "I don't want to look at a topic from just one perspective," he says. "I want to look at the complexities, to come up with a piece of writing in greater dimensions."[1]

In the concluding pages of "The Keel of Lake Dickey," McPhee is unequivocal. He does not believe that the dam should be built and with sharp sarcasm and passionate prose, he says so. "Panic about the Arabs brought all this on, but deeper than the panic is an apparent belief that it is the right of people to have all the electric power they can afford to buy, with the subsidiary right of squandering it when and how they please and of buying it at the same rate at any time of the day. We throw away more power than a Dickey Dam could ever give us, by ten times ten times ten. We throw it away in kilowatt-years. And anyone who would do that would throw away a river" (176). Such bluntness is rare in McPhee's work, but the conclusion seems less a jeremiad than a plaintive cry. And, in a certain respect, the editorial qualities of the story are balanced by the expected McPhee characterizations—of the young Lev Byrd, Admiral Richard Byrd's grandson; or Tom Cabot, seventy-eight, fighting cancer but still able to engage in a white-water canoe trip and to demonstrate a buoyant sense of humor.

In addition, McPhee is capable of showing that he can see the comic side of his experience. He recounts the friendly competition among the travelers concerning their outdoor equipment—their Duluth packs, their reflector ovens, their Buck knives, their Allagash Dishwasher's bags. McPhee offers a set piece about L. L. Bean's store in Freeport, Maine, that de-mythifies one part of the outdoor religion:

If you travel in bush Alaska, you find Bean's catalogues in cabin after cabin there, and Bean's boots and garments on the people. Most transactions are by mail, but the home store, in Freeport, in Cumberland County, is open twenty-four hours a day seven days a week. I know people who have gone shopping at Bean's at four o'clock in the morning and have reported themselves to have been by no means the only customers there. The store is a rampant mutation of New England connective architecture—an awkward, naive building, seeming to consist of many wooden boxes stacked atop one another and held together by steel exterior trusses. There is nothing naive about the cash register. Sometimes it is necessary to go off to the woods for indefinite periods to recover from a visit to Bean's. (141–2)

The Control of Nature

McPhee's attitudes toward nature are developed more deeply and, perhaps, more ingeniously in *The Control of Nature,* his amalgamation of three stories about people engaged in battles with elemental forces in the world around them. Similar to the origins of many of his stories, the catalyst for writing it was serendipity. His daughter Sarah was taking a course on the novelist Walker Percy at Harvard, and she wanted to go to Louisiana, Walker Percy country, on vacation with her father. McPhee took his daughter, but he took his own side trip into the swamp, which led to the idea about human attempts to control the natural world.[2]

In the opening section, "Atchafalaya," McPhee shows his admiration for both nature and human nature. This section is the story of efforts to control the Mississippi River or, more specifically, to control the draw of the Atchafalaya, the major distributary of the Mississippi. The Atchafalaya has a steeper gradient than the Mississippi and cuts a more direct route to the Gulf. It is natural for the Mississippi to seek the most direct route to the Gulf. Each decade since 1860 the distributary drew off more water from its source than it had in the decade before, and if nothing had been done the Atchafalaya would have taken all of the Mississippi and "itself become the master stream" (*Control,* 5).

Too much hangs in the balance—towns and industry—for the government to allow the Atchafalaya to have its way. Therefore, as McPhee says, "Nature, in this place, had become an enemy of the state" (7). The battle lines are drawn. It is a war between two strong forces. The one, nature, moves inexorably in one direction, fueled by immutable laws. The other, humankind, proceeds from pride and imagination, aided by science and technology. Such a conflict seems to be the stuff of either tragedy or great achievement. It is a battle in which McPhee seems to respect both nature's awesome, inevitable power and man's stubborn, Promethean ingenuity.

In 1963 the U.S. Army Corps of Engineers built a weir known as Old River Control Structure. The function of the dam at Old River is to maintain a steady thirty-percent flow into the Atchafalaya and to ensure that the rest of the water of the Mississippi continues to flow unimpeded toward New Orleans three hundred miles away. If not for the Old River Control Structure the course of the Mississippi would change, leaving the cities along the way literally high and dry. According to McPhee, leaving the Atchafalaya to its own course would mean the end of Baton Rouge. It would also turn New Orleans into New Gomorrah, "its fresh water gone, its harbor a silt bar, its economy disconnected from inland commerce" (6).

Over the passage of time the Mississippi River has changed course many times and transformed the shape of the land around it. Earliest settlers just moved when the river decided to impose its whims. More recent settlements have been more obstinate. "From the beginnings of settlement, failure was the par expectation with respect to the river—a fact generally masked by the powerful fabric of ambition that impelled people to build towns and cities where almost any camper would be loath to pitch a tent" (31). Once ambition had created the likes of Vicksburg, there was no choice but to stand and fight—as General Thomas Sands of the U. S. Army Corps of Engineers says, "Man against nature. That's what life's all about" (20).

This is the sort of epic battle—between humankind and nature—that McPhee seems perfectly suited to dramatize. He is reporter in the field, noting casualties, acts of heroism, and moments of irony. One of civilization's first tactics to control the Mississippi was to build levees. Slaves with wheelbarrows, then immigrants with shovels, then mule-drawn scrapers, and finally bulldozers and earth-moving machines built earthen walls higher and higher. Each time a flood came, and they came with the regularity of an enemy who would not understand the word *surrender*, higher levees were built. The levees were compounding the problem that they were meant to alleviate, though. "The more the levees confined the river, the more destructive it became when they failed. A place where water broke through was known as a crevasse—a source of terror no less effective than a bursting dam—and the big ones were memorialized, like other great disasters, in a series of proper names: the Macarty Crevasse (1816), the Sauve Crevasse (1849)" (35).

McPhee says that although the levees were often compared to the Great Wall of China, they more closely resembled the Maginot Line (46). The higher the levees became the more powerful the shackled Mississippi grew. McPhee quotes Mark Twain in *Life on the Mississippi* to support his idea that the struggle against the river might have had all the elements of the story of Sisyphus to it. "One who knows the Mississippi will promptly aver—not aloud but to himself—that ten thousand River Commissions, with the mines of the world at their back, cannot tame that lawless stream, cannot curb it or confine it, cannot say to it, 'Go here,' or 'Go there,' and make it obey; cannot save a shore which it has sentenced; cannot bar its path with an obstruction which it will not tear down, dance over, laugh at" (39). The levees had more than the Mississippi River to contend with. They had human nature to deal with as well. If a levee across the river failed, that meant that the farmland on the opposite side was safer; therefore, people had to patrol the levees so that saboteurs did not dynamite a neighbor's protection.

Eventually, officials realized that levees alone were not enough to attempt to control the river. Spillways and weirs would acknowledge the superiority of the natural force of the river and give it back some of its freedom, in controlled tons of water. McPhee describes men like Norris F. Rabalais and Leroy Dugas who would watch and wait like sentinels along a war-marked border. General Thomas Sands, looking "somewhat less martial than most English teachers," is the water czar (66), dedicated to doing battle with the enemy, the Atchafalaya, "those rippling syllables" that to McPhee symbolize the phrase "control of nature" . . . "The word will now come to mind more or less in echo of any struggle against natural forces—heroic or venal, rash or well advised—when human beings conscript themselves to fight against the earth, to take what is not given, to rout the destroying enemy, to surround the base of Mt. Olympus demanding and expecting the surrender of the gods" (69).

McPhee portrays the tenacity and courage of individuals like Dugas and Rabalais, and he also dramatizes the collective perseverance of a town like Morgan City, surrounded by a twenty-two-foot wall and in the direct path of the planned flood. "Damocles would not have been so lonely had he lived in Morgan City. In a proportion inverse to the seawall's great size, the seawall betokens a vulnerability the like of which is hard to find so far from a volcano" (79). It is hard to imagine that levees and weirs and flood control structures will be enough to stave off the river. Even the two-million-dollar picket boat *Kent,* eighty-five feet long and with radar beams and twin nine-hundred-horse diesel engines, seems a frail adversary, as it stands "alert to everything that moves in the river, including catfish" (92). But, nevertheless, there it floats, near Old River Control, with its expensive technological equipment and a fifteen-inch bamboo pole, too.

The volcano that McPhee mentions in regard to the vulnerability of Morgan City is the topic of the second section of the book, "Cooling the Lava." On 23 January 1973, a fissure opened in the outskirts of Heimaey, a community of five thousand people on an island off the mainland of Iceland. The volcanic eruption lasted five and a half months, until July 1973. During that time the eruption dropped "a curtain of lava five hundred feet high and a mile long" (97) into the sky above the town. The two-mile-long fissure put ash in the streets "dense enough to drive on, even where it was fifteen and twenty feet deep" (132).

This section of the book, like the other two parts, suggests that nature always has the edge. As McPhee rhetorically asks, "Who could not agree that the odds seemed to favor nature" (107)? In this war it would be arrogance not to recognize the power of the opponent. "On the eleventh day of the eruption, ash came down with winter rain in a mixture so dense that a person on a sidewalk could not see across the street. Bombs were falling through the ash and rain. Flowing lava, moving north and east, had by now extended the island about two thousand feet. . . . The volcano's murmurings became out-and-out explosions, so violent they shook the town. . . . The liquid sprays of lava reached heights around a thousand feet" (111{en2}. Inevitably, these are wars that humankind engages in rarely and never permanently win. McPhee cites Pompeii and numerous examples from Hawaii to make this point. There is even a risk in winning. By using water to create a chilled margin, a water-hardened territory, had the scientists "actually caused the newly appearing lava to turn left and overrun the city" (142)? There are heroes in this war—Thorbjorn Sigurgeirsson or Sveinn Eiriksson—but, ultimately, there is no clear winner, nor can there ever be. There will always be stubborn individuals, heroic, at times foolish, and indomitable nature. "As Thorbjorn is the first to suggest . . . the true extent of the victory will never be known—the role of luck being unassessable, the effects of intervention being ultimately incalculable, and the assertion that people can stop a volcano being hubris enough to provoke a new eruption" (179).

The third section, "Los Angeles Against the Mountains," begins with a long anecdote about a family named the Genofiles and their frightening encounter with a debris flow. It is a suspenseful tale, as taut with tension as a piece of adventure fiction—but it is a true story of the Genofiles in the winter of 1978 as they watched in horror as their home in the San Gabriel Mountains filled up, to their children's chins, with mud and debris. As McPhee explains, debris flows look a bit like fresh concrete and consist of water mixed with a great deal of solid material— dirt and rocks, limbs and trees, and even a Chevrolet or two. In the case of the Genofiles, the debris flow brought tons of mud and thirteen cars, five of which landed in their swimming pool. The Genofiles's story has a happy ending, but McPhee recounts some of the disasters and deaths so that their good luck (and Bob Genofile's building skill) are set into relief against the darker possibilities.

McPhee makes it clear that Los Angeles has to pick and choose its fights with nature, for there are plenty of places for the city to draw a line in the sand. There are droughts, earthquakes, and floods. The rugged terrain of the San Gabriel Mountains is just one battleground but the one McPhee chose in this instance. Nature, whether it be the Mississippi River or a volcano in Iceland, is an awesome force, and when human beings get too close to the source of its power—the banks of the river or on the edges of the mountain—they must deal with the threat.

Those who live in the mountains above Los Angeles must, in one way or another, face the possibility of disaster at any time. That could mean thousands of tons of mud and boulders sliding and crashing down the mountainside, through their homes. It could mean coffins slipping down the hills at midnight like a scene out of *Poltergeist,* or it could mean someone's bedroom sailing down the driveway on top of the family station wagon like a remake of a Buster Keaton film. The people who choose to live in such areas must face the potential consequences of the fire-flood sequence on the natural world. Debris flows have multiple causes. The earthquakes in the area create a lot of broken rock. Chaparral, one of the most flammable vegetations in the world, is a part of the landscape and subject to inevitable, periodic fires. Chaparral fires burn as if they were "soaked with gasoline" (210). Chaparral litter creates a soil that is essentially waterproof. The rains that come, especially an intense storm, one that produces as it did in 1978 an inch and a half of rain in twenty-five minutes, force the loose rocks and debris down the mountainside with the force of a flash flood.

Those who live in the face of such danger have to have "heroic chutz-pah" (265) and, perhaps, a sense of irony. When the Genofiles survived their battle with a debris flow by a mere few inches and decided to rebuild his house, what his men call "the fort" (186), the local chamber of commerce gave them the Beautification Award for Best Home, an award given for "good maintenance" and a "sense of drama" (202). In the midst of this battle with nature, McPhee stands on an ironic footing of his own. He respects nature's destructive power and breathtaking beauty. He seems aware of humankind's hubris and blindness, as well as its ingenuity and courage. He stands between the two to tell the story. At one point, as he ventures from the main path to explore some of the geological implications of the story, he says, "It had not been my purpose, in pursuing the present theme, to get into the deep geology. I meant to roam the mountains and the mountain front with foresters and engineers, to talk to people living on the urban edge, to interview people who sell the edge—a foreign correspondent covering the battle from behind both lines. But not beneath them" (224).

McPhee's sympathies, it seems, are always with the intrepid, the knowledgeable, the dextrous, and therefore he gravitates toward such ordinary heroes, but he values the truth of the tale and will tell it, no matter what pain it causes or what position he must find to discover the heart of the story. He may sit in the bow of the canoe or with blistered feet follow his subjects up an incline or he may just sit. "Needle grass went through my trousers. The heads of needle grass detach from the stalks and have the barbed design of arrows. They were going by the quiver into my butt but I still preferred to sit. It was the better posture for writing notes" (207). Many readers feel that the three stories in *The Control of Nature* bear witness to the triumph of nature over human engineering. Rather, it seems to me that the stories of human endurance, of gritty perseverance, balance those reflecting nature's preeminence. McPhee seems most respectful of those individuals who realistically confront the breathtaking and often backbreaking force of nature and take their chances anyway. He is also aware of humankind's arrogance and its innocence in its attempts to control the uncontrollable. McPhee, the artist who in a sense controls nature by recreating it in narratives, strives to write, it seems, with equal respect and attention about Nature and human nature as well.

Annals of the Former World

For more than a decade McPhee worked on his geological tetralogy, gathered under the title *Annals of the Former World*. In 1981 he published *Basin and Range*, in 1982 *In Suspect Terrain*, in 1986 *Rising from the Plains*, and finally in 1993 *Assembling California.* The quartet is his biggest work and perhaps the most difficult challenge that he has taken on as a writer. In a 1994 interview he discussed the special problems involved in such a project. "The geology pieces were really, really difficult. *Basin and Range* was the hardest of all because it was the first of those geology pieces. I was in over my head and I kept saying, 'What am I doing? Why am I doing this? How did I get into this?' more intensely than I had done with anything else. With the geology, I made the unhappy discovery that you couldn't just learn a little corner of it, use it for journalistic purposes, and then go on. The stuff is just too much this-related-to-that-related-to-the-other-thing. You had to know it."[3] What started as a two-day project that was to turn into a brief, unsigned piece for the *New Yorker*'s "The Talk of the Town" section became a decade of work and four books. In the third book in the series, *Rising from the Plains,* McPhee acknowledges the necessity of comprehensiveness: There is, he says, "no good way to comprehend any one aspect of geology without studying the wider matrix in which it rests" (*Plains,* 125).

Individual books in the geological sequence and his entire work on geology have had to endure a few critical tremors. Stephen Jay Gould, writing in the *New York Review of Books,* says that McPhee has been "beguiled by the mystique of field work. . . . This mythology leads to serious, but unfortunately conventional, misrepresentations of the past, a tradition that McPhee follows in the historical section of his work."[4] Robert D. Hatcher, writing in *Natural History,* suggests that the danger McPhee runs in his work on geology is to allow the story to get "bogged down in jargon."[5] And Beaufort Cranford, in the *Detroit News,* may more directly state some readers' misgivings about the geological theme, "Not even McPhee, alas, could consistently elevate that dismal subject above avalanching tedium."[6]

But many readers and critics see the tetralogy as an example of McPhee's best writing. Amy Meeker, in *Atlantic,* says that *Basin and Range* "abounds in McPhee's characteristic good humor and his instinct for the delightfully incongruous yet telling detail." Meeker goes on to say that "the language of geology becomes [him]" and that the book is "a multilayered narrative that is both lucid and lyrical."[7] Michiko Kakutani, writing on the front page of the *New York Times Book Review,* said that McPhee in *In Suspect Terrain* sets himself the daunting task of reading "the biography of the earth." Although Kakutani admits that the subject of geology is "more resistant than usual to his civilizing prose," she recognizes that geology is also a logical topic for the writer to be drawn toward—for it represents "the confluence of his love of nature with his interest in science."[8] W. Ross Winterowd feels that a book like *Rising from the Plains* is "literature of very high quality."[9] And Barbara Lounsberry sees McPhee aspiring toward the philosophical limits of nonfiction in a work like *Basin and Range:* he attempts "to expand our comprehension of ourselves in time."[10] In a sense, Paul Zweig is reflecting on the same idea when he writes in 1981: "McPhee conveys the excitement of the geologist's interpretive jags, his struggle to divert the cozy prospect of human language to a new task: the description of events so glued in the slowness of mineral time that they annihilate the scale of our lives and furnish convincing images of eternity."[11] It is McPhee's good-humored professorial demeanor that comes across in the geology quartet, as it does in many of his other books. Zweig compares McPhee to Montaigne, for both men, Zweig says, have "the same sort of miscellaneous temperament, the same fascination with odd bits of knowledge."[12]

Basin and Range

Basin and Range, like the other three books on geology, is concerned with what McPhee calls deep time. Following a pattern from his other works, in the geology quartet McPhee takes on the role of student who pays careful attention to the mentor-guide that he finds along the way. For the rest of us McPhee takes precise, poetic notes. In each book an eminent geologist leads the way. In *Basin and Range* McPhee's principal teacher is Kenneth Deffeyes, in *In Suspect Terrain* it is Anita Harris, in *Rising from the Plains* it is David Love, and in *Assembling California* it is Eldridge Moores. Each of these "teachers" is knowledgeable, passionately involved in his or her discipline, and each has a similar story to tell—a story about time, time that stretches out for millions and millions of years, time that reaches beyond the human capacity to imagine it. In each of the four books the hero, ultimately, is not an individual geologist but the earth itself.

McPhee's interest in geology may have its roots in his activities at Camp Keewaydin when he was a young boy, but the fact that geologists, as one scientist in *In Suspect Terrain* says, are engaged in legitimized tourism, may also appeal to McPhee. Karen Kleinspehn, a geology student in *Basin and Range,* early in the book states her motives for studying the earth. She may be voicing some of McPhee's motives as well: "There's a little bit of the humanities that creeps into geology, and that's why I am in it. You can't prove things as rigorously as physicists or chemists do" (12). As McPhee makes clear, ninety-nine percent of the picture is missing—"melted or dissolved, torn down, washed away, broken to bits, to become something else in the Picture" (79). David Love, of the Geological Survey, thinks the science of geology is like the "blind men feeling the elephant" (80)—each one will come up with a different large picture based upon the piece he touches. To use Barbara Lounsberry's metaphor in discussing McPhee's work, the geology books allow him to ponder the largest circle, perhaps, that is available to a reporter. McPhee's focus on the earth—on the changes that occur invisible to the human eye fixed on smaller things and quicker shifts—is a focus on the eternal. Placed in the context of geologic change, humankind's history seems fleeting. Human history is a fraction of the story, and in that perspective—the Industrial Revolution occurring in one-fortieth of a second in terms of the time of the earth's story—some of humankind's sense of self-importance and invincibility should diminish. "The human consciousness may have begun to leap and boil some sunny day in the Pleistocene, but the race by and large has retained the essence of its sense of animal time. People think in five generations—two ahead, two behind—with heavy concentration on the one in the middle. . . . The human mind may not have evolved enough to be able to comprehend deep time. It may only be able to measure it" (127).

Understanding the enormous range of deep time is both humbling and ennobling. For geologists, a million years is a very short time span. Geologists must turn their minds to the planet's time scale. As one geologist says, "For me, it is almost unconscious now and is a kind of companionship with the earth" (129). There is an ecological and philosophical resonance in such statements, a spiritual dimension. "If you free yourself from the conventional reaction to a quantity like a million years, you free yourself a bit from the boundaries of human time. And then in a way you do not live at all, but in another way you live forever" (129). The theme that McPhee suggests is that a knowledge of the history of the earth, its slow but inevitable changes, will allow us to read the narrative of prehuman history.

In the geology quartet, McPhee cuts a swath across the continent, more or less following Route 80, and he also travels imaginatively around the globe, alluding to geological features on other parts of the planet; but he begins *Basin and Range* in a specific location, close to his home in Princeton. He went with Karen Kleinspehn to the west apron of the George Washington Bridge, "at 73 degrees 57 minutes and 53

seconds west longitude and 40 degrees 51 minutes and 14 seconds
north latitude" (3). McPhee says that these coordinates are only a "tem-
porary description . . . as if for a boat on the sea" (3), for everything on
the earth is moving. Nothing suggests McPhee's point better than his
statement "The summit of Mt. Everest is marine limestone" (183).

The story of geological deep time in *Basin and Range* merges with the
profile of Kenneth Deffeyes and the story of the development of geological science since the eighteenth century. It is the history of James Hutton and his *Theory of the Earth* in 1785. It is Hutton's phrase "annals of a
former world" that serves as the overarching title for McPhee's rumina-
tions on geology. Hutton argued that the earth's mineral surface had
been shaped by the slowest of geological activity. Each rock, every
mountain, range, ocean, and cliff became a story that could be read. For
McPhee, a man who sees interesting texts everywhere—in orange
groves, around dirigibles, in a produce market—this sense of the textu-
ality of the world must seem the right theory, indeed. In the nineteenth
century Charles Lyell advanced Hutton's theory of deep time and slow
change for the earth. Darwin read Lyell admiringly and moved forward
in his theory of evolution. It was not until the early 1960s, however,
that, as Kenneth Deffeyes says, "a change as profound as Darwinian
evolution, or Newtonian or Einsteinian physics" (177) occurred, and
between 1957 and 1967 plate tectonics theory became widely accepted:

> The story is that everything is moving, that the outlines of the continents
> by and large have nothing to do with these motions, that "continental
> drift" is actually a misnomer, that only the world picture according to
> Marco Polo makes much sense in the old-time browns and greens and
> Rand McNally blues. The earth is at present divided into some twenty
> crustal segments called plates. Plate boundaries miscellaneously run
> through the continents, and down the middle of the oceans. The plates are
> thin and rigid, like pieces of eggshell. . . . It is the plates that move. They
> all move. They move in varying directions and at varying speeds. (178–9)

The theory of plate tectonics, according to McPhee, "assembled numerous disparate phenomena into a single narrative" (180). This, in essence,
is what McPhee attempts to do in his tetralogy on geology. *Basin and
Range,* as the first book in the quartet, sets the stage by giving a sense of
the larger picture, a glimpse of the recent history of the science. It also
gives the reader an idea of the format for the other books.

Despite the difficulties a reader must face with any of McPhee's geology books, *Basin and Range,* and the tetralogy in general, offers a great

deal for the effort. First, the tetralogy offers a wealth of information on the moving and shifting earth. Second, nestled gently between bits of geological jargon is the expected McPhee prose, lyrical and poetic: "I have seen the salt lake incredibly beautiful in winter dusk under snow-streamer curtains of cloud moving fast through the sky, with the wall of the Wasatch a deep rose and the lake islands rising from what seemed to be rippled slate" (63). *Basin and Range* and the other geology books offer an epic picture, if not an epic cast of human characters. There are portraits of individuals, though, and amusing anecdotes, and some high adventure—stories of silver mining and earthquakes. There is even, in *Basin and Range,* a UFO sighting by journalist and scientist.

In Suspect Terrain

The second volume in the tetralogy, *In Suspect Terrain,* published in 1983, is what Barbara Lounsberry calls "McPhee's Thoreauvian minority report on plate-tectonics theory."[13] *In Suspect Terrain* is linked directly to *Basin and Range* in terms of its emphasis on the revolutionary plate tectonics theory. In contrast to *Basin and Range,* which summarizes plate tectonics theory, *In Suspect Terrain* challenges the universal truth of the theory. It is like the deconstructive other to the first volume in the quartet. Specifically, geologist Anita Harris worries that "the theory is taught perhaps too glibly in schools" (*In Suspect,* 5). Harris considers herself the devil's advocate of plate tectonics theory (210). Although she does not reject the theory out of hand (121), she is certainly not one of its advocates. She is most closely aligned to her second husband, Leonard Harris, also a geologist. "With regard to plate tectonics, he looked upon himself as a missionary of contrary opinion—not flat and rigid but selective, where he had knowledge to contribute. His wife compared him to Martin Luther, nailing theses to the door of the castle church" (132). Harris believes that plate theory is often carelessly applied, and when some facts do not fit the theory, then it is a simple matter of "If at first it doesn't fit, fit, fit again" (135). Toward the end of *In Suspect Terrain* Harris makes her point straightforwardly:

> To many problems, plate tectonics is not the only solution. Often, it's a lazy man's out. It's a way of saying, 'I don't have to think any further.' It's a way of getting out of a problem. The geology has refuted plate-tectonic interpretations time and again in the Appalachians. Geology often refutes plate tectonics. So the plate-tectonics boys tend to ignore the data. The horror is the ignoring of basic facts, not bothering to be

constrained by data. . . . There are a lot of people out there in the profession like me who don't believe much of it. (209–10)

Harris, nee Fishman, grew up in the slums of Williamsburg Brooklyn. For her, geology was a means of escape. "I knew that if I went into geology I would never have to live in New York City," she said. "It was a way to get out" (7). With some trepidation, more than twenty-five years after her escape from a Brooklyn tenement, Harris takes McPhee on a tour of her old neighborhood, of the pitted outwash plains of Brooklyn, which means "broken land" (20). Geologists like Anita Harris have a kinship with poets and historians. They see what was once there. They imagine worlds now gone. Where the average eye sees abandoned buildings, garbage-strewn highways, and empty lots, the geologist sees ancient tidal flats, and terminal moraines. Near Coney Island, where she was born, Harris, in the prose of McPhee, sees a geologist's landscape. "The beach itself, with its erratic sands, was the extremity of the outwash plain. The Wisconsinan ice sheet, arriving from the north, had come over the city not from New England, as one might guess, but primarily from New Jersey, whose Hudson River counties lie due north of Manhattan. Big boulders from the New Jersey Palisades are strewn about in Central Park, and more of the same diabase is scattered through Brooklyn. The ice wholly covered the Bronx and Manhattan, and its broad snout moved across Astoria, Maspeth, Williamsburg, and Bedford-Stuyvesant before sliding to a stop in Flatbush" (24). As a child Harris journeyed from her home, across the Williamsburg Bridge, and into Manhattan. The study of geology was a way for her to keep walking, beyond Williamsburg and Manhattan, a way to be "paid 'for walking around in mountains'" (7). McPhee sketches her childhood in Brooklyn, and he traces the geology of the area at the same time. He runs these parallel lines of biography and geology as he heads west on Interstate 80 through her graduate study in Indiana and Ohio, in the process discussing glaciers and the Ice Age, various scientific debates, and the dizzying perspectives of geologic time.

Rising from the Plains

It is in the third book in the quartet, *Rising from the Plains,* that McPhee seems to most artfully blend the story of the geologist with the narrative of geology. The book is concerned with Rocky Mountain geology and the preeminent Rocky Mountain geologist, David Love. The book begins a sort of "duet" played between the lucid prose of McPhee and selected, lyrical passages from the unpublished journal of Ethel Waxham, David Love's mother.[14] Partly through Ethel Waxham's journal, from which he takes the title for his book, McPhee repeats the story of the pioneer spirit in the West. Miss Waxham arrived in Wyoming in 1905, a recent graduate of Wellesley College in Massachusetts, her Phi Beta Kappa key still dangling from her neck, to teach school in "a log cabin on Twin Creek near the mouth of Skull Gulch" (*Plains,* 30). It was not an easy place for man or woman, but perhaps especially difficult for someone whose field was classical studies. Nevertheless, Ethel Waxham proved herself to be smart, intuitive, adaptable, and tough as the wild country she entered. She is as vivid as a character in one of Willa Cather's prairie novels.

Her story was also the story of John Love, a Scottsman with a twinkle in his eye and the kind of sinewy body and spirit that would make it possible for him to sleep out, in one stretch, under no shelter for seven years (35). John Love was a self-made man, although he came from good stock: His father was a physician, professional photographer, and lecturer; his uncle was the environmentalist John Muir. John Love did well in the ranching business, eventually making a small fortune, losing it, and making it over again. Ethel Waxham was attracted less to his success, it seems, than to the "twinkle in his voice as well as in his eyes" (35). He spoke with a "wooly Midlothian accent" (34), and he was able to "draw Scottish poems out of the air like bolts of silk" (78). It took him five years to convince Ethel to marry him, but in 1910 she did, and they spent their life together on a ranch in the Wind River Basin, a "plain country with gently swelling hills" (42). As Evan S. Connell said in a review of *Rising from the Plains,* the Loves "homesteaded on Muskrat Creek at a time closer in spirit to King Arthur's court than to present-day America."[15]

David Love grew up on that ranch, "drawn to be a geologist in much the same way that someone growing up in Gloucester, Massachusetts, would be drawn to be a fisherman" (103). He was taught at home by his mother, reading Shakespeare and Thoreau. At nine years old he read his mother's copy of LeConte's *Elements of Geology,* and he understood it because, as he says, "After all, we could see it out in front of us" (106). Love became enamored of Wyoming, a state that "contains a disproportionate percentage of American geology" (26). As McPhee says, "A geologist who grew up in Wyoming would have something of everything" (27).

With a contrapuntal movement, *Rising from the Plains* moves back and forth between human time and geological time. As McPhee criss-crosses the state with his subject-guide David Love, he weaves a narrative that joins the best of what he does as a writer—informing, describing, entertaining—a knitting together of dramatic profile and scientific exposition. Seamlessly, he joins the pioneer story of John Love and Ethel Waxham, anecdotes about Butch Cassidy and other outlaws, and the story of David Love and the mysteries of geology.

David Love's relationship to Wyoming seems to be similar to the perspective of Gretel Ehrlich, whom Annie Dillard called the Whitman of present-day Wyoming. In her book on Wyoming, *The Solace of Open Spaces,* Ehrlich wrote:

> From the clayey soil of northern Wyoming is mined bentonite, which is used as a filler in candy, gum, and lipstick. We Americans are great on fillers, as if what we have, what we are, is not enough. We have a cultural tendency toward denial, but, being affluent, we strangle ourselves with what we can buy. We have only to look at the houses we build to see how we build *against* space, the way we drink against pain and loneliness. We fill up space as if it were a pie shell, with things whose opacity further obstructs our ability to see what is already there.[16]

Like Ehrlich, Love "cares passionately about Wyoming" (180), and as McPhee makes clear, Love is the kind of man who understands a landscape with "a space so great that you can stand on a hilltop and see not only what Jim Bridger saw but also—through dimming tracts of time—what no one saw" (180).

Ironically, Love, who has "the geologic map of Wyoming in his head" (23), becomes an unwilling assistant in the uranium industry's hold on the state. A report he drafts for the U.S. Geological Survey makes him "in both a specific and a general sense, the discoverer of uranium in commercial quantity in Wyoming and the progenitor of the Wyoming uranium industry" (209). Love reflects on this fact one day when he and McPhee stand on the crest of the Gas Hills, "where fifty open-pit uranium mines" (210) surround them. The ranch that Love grew up on near Muskrat Creek has experienced a seven-hundred percent increase in the uranium level. Like Ted Taylor, then, Love is haunted by some of the effects of his own genius. "In the Gas Hills, as we traced with our eyes his journeys to Green Mountain, he said, 'You can see it was quite a trek by wagon. Am I troubled? Yes. At places like this, we thought we were doing a great service to the nation. In hindsight, we do not know if we were performing a service or a disservice. Sometimes I think I might regret it. Yes. It's close to home' " (214).

As Barbara Lounsberry points out, despite any connection to destruction in the environment, David Love, like Ted Taylor or David Brower, is one of McPhee's representative men, a man who "represents a point of view at odds with his time."[17] Once Love retires, the U.S. Geological Survey will shut down the regional field office that symbolizes his type of geology. As McPhee says, "Love has become vestigial in the structure of the Survey" (124). Like other things vestigial, Love is a reminder of something that will be lost. Perhaps McPhee might be suggesting that a man like David Love is that rare sort of individual who can connect human time and deep time, who can track the mystery of the earth with intelligence and humility. "We crossed the North Platte, climbed some long grades, examined a few roadcuts, and pulled off on the shoulder at Rawlins to absorb, in the multiple exposures of the Rawlins Uplift, its comprehensive spread of time—Rawlins, where his mother had boarded the stage north, three-quarters of a century before" (77). And McPhee might also be implying that the deepest meaning of *vestigial,* a meaning that itself has become a vestige, archaic, may apply to David Love and the story of the geology of Wyoming—that geologists like Love leave a "footprint, a track" it would be wise to follow.

Assembling California

In the final book in the geology quartet, *Assembling California,* published in 1993, McPhee takes his narrative as far at it can go west on Interstate 80. As McPhee establishes early in the final volume of the tetralogy, the series of geology books might not have a linear progress in geographic terms, but the quartet was always "thematically . . . aimed at California" (*Assembling,* 9). In the process of representing "the consensual biography of the earth" (9), his purpose, from the beginning, had been to describe "not only the rock exposed in roadcuts— and the regional geologies into which the roadcuts would serve as windows—but also the geologists themselves" (8). It is Kenneth Deffeyes, his expert-guide from *Basin and Range,* who tells McPhee that he needs a California geologist, a tectonicist like Eldridge Moores, editor of *Geology* magazine from 1981 to 1988 and professor of geology at the University of California at Davis. It seems appropriate to have a tectonicist to lead the way toward the western edge of the continent, for California was fashioned by earthquakes:

For an extremely large percentage of the history of the world, there was
no California. . . . The continent ended far to the east, the continental
shelf as well. Where California has come to be, there was only blue sea
reaching down some miles to ocean-crustal rock, which was moving, as it
does, into subduction zones to be consumed. . . . Then, a piece at a
time—according to present theory—parts began to assemble. An island
arc here, a piece of continent there—a Japan at a time, a New Zealand, a
Madagascar—came crunching in upon the continent and have thus far
adhered. . . . In 1906, the jump of the great earthquake—the throw, the
offset, the maximum amount of local displacement as one plate moved
with respect to the other—was something like twenty feet. The dynam-
ics that have pieced together the whole of California have consisted of
tens of thousands of earthquakes as great as that—tens of thousands of
examples of what people like to singularize as "the big one"—and many
millions of earthquakes of lesser magnitude. (5–6)

In 1970 Moores published an essay in *Nature* that was the first article
to suggest the "collisional assembly of California" (108). *Assembling California* moves to the brink of things in two respects—to the edge of the
continent and to the climax of plate tectonics theory. The theory of plate
tectonics has been the controlling feature that has "shaped the over-all
structure" (9) of the tetralogy, and the story of earthquakes is a revela-
tory moment in that narrative, a point where human and geological
time intersect.

Like plate tectonics itself, McPhee's writing on geology could be
described as "structure on the move" (27). In *Assembling California,* he
moves even more freely from one point to another, geographically and
topically, than he does in the first three books. He travels out of the
realm of Route 80 and the United States, following his guide to Greece
and Cyprus. Along the way there are tales of Thermopylae, Cypriot
ministers of the interior, and Macedonian women who show their affection by spitting on the Moores's children—all interspersed with information about copper mining on Cyprus, gold mining in California, or
the importance of the ophiolitic sequence to the theory of plate tectonics.

As with the first three geology works, *Assembling California* presents
the reader with some difficult linguistic terrain. McPhee barely pauses
for breath at times over breccias, xenoliths, andesites, gabbros, and
taphrogeosynclines. For instance, here is a passage from the beginning
of the book: "If bands of phyllites and folded metasediments happen to
be there, up they go as part of the mountains. If serpentinized peri-

dotites and gold-bearing gravels happen to be there, up they go as part of the mountains. If a great granite batholith happens to be there, up it goes as part of the mountains. And while everything is going up it is being eroded as well, by water and (sometimes) ice. Cirques are cut, and U-shaped valleys, ravines, minarets" (19). But he can as readily make poetry out of the scientific terminology as geo-cobble. A bit further along in the story he offers this description: "It was fine-grained diabase, in magnification asparkle with crystals—free-form, asymmetrical, improvisational plagioclase crystals bestrewn against a field of dark pyroxene" (76).

McPhee, like Moores it seems, is a man who "variously fizzes and clicks" (76) over unusual rock forms. As geologists see it, the earth is on the move, and McPhee's narrative mirrors that movement, shifting and sliding from Moores's growing up in the mountains of Arizona and being part of a family that owned a small mine—his family depended for its livelihood on the yield from Gladiator Mine in rural Arizona—to anecdotes glinting with the history of gold fever in the West. For Moores, gold mining was a dirty, dreary business, and like Anita Harris who sought to escape Brooklyn through geology, he wanted away from that life he grew up knowing.

The anecdotes that McPhee recounts about the mid-nineteenth-century story of gold mining are dramatic and violent: "In four months in Mokelumne Hill, there is a murder every week. In the absence of law, lynching is common. . . . When a mob forgets to tie the hands of a condemned man and he clutches the rope above him, someone beats his hands with a pistol until he lets go. . . . A young miner in Bear River kills an older man. A tribunal offers him death or banishment. He selects death, explaining that he is from Kentucky. In Kentucky, that would be the honorable thing to do" (59). In mining, as in earthquakes, human time and geological time intersect briefly. Only occasionally, as Moores explains to McPhee, do the two time scales coincide (48), and it is essential, both McPhee and Moores feel, to get across a sense of the slow rate of geological time. By focusing on some of the points of convergence, McPhee dramatizes the relationship between the two perspectives.

McPhee views the slow shifts in the earth's physical features like a movie maker who filmed a narrative frame by frame and then showed the film speeded up to fit his audience's human sense of chronology. "When continents collided, Africa docked with, among other places, the Old South. About a hundred and fifty million years later, when Africa departed, it apparently left a large piece of Florida, which is now covered with what Moores calls 'a lot of modern limestones that developed on top of the Appalachian suture, which can be traced seismologically under northern Florida and off into the continental shelf " (207). McPhee summarizes some ideas about the earth's changes generated by plate tectonics theory. Southeastern Staten Island was once part of Europe, Boston once a part of Africa, the northwest Highlands of Scotland once a piece of America. Vancouver Island came from somewhere near the latitude of Bolivia. Chile and western Peru may have come from somewhere in the South Pacific. Laguna Beach and Pasadena are fourteen miles closer today than they were two million years ago (208, 219, 224, 266).

The most dramatic example of the earth's movement is an earthquake. The culminating point in the plot of *Assembling California* is San Francisco, the American city that has become synonymous with the word *earthquake*. It is the place in McPhee's narrative where human time and geological time nick one another, specifically in the form of the 1989 earthquake that struck the Bay Area. The story of California is the story of earthquakes, and the story of earthquakes is plate tectonics. "California has not assembled on the creep. Great earthquakes are all over the geology. A big one will always be in the offing. The big one is plate tectonics" (253). McPhee's description of the San Andreas Fault, "like a fresh scar on a President's belly" (254), joins the timely and the timeless and in the same breath suggests the gap between the two time periods, human and geological frames of reference.

It seems appropriate structurally and thematically that McPhee concludes *Assembling California* with a series of dizzying images of the most recent quake in the Bay Area:

> In a fourth-floor apartment, a woman in her kitchen has been cooking Rice-A-Roni. She has put on long johns and a sweatshirt and turned on the television to watch the World Series. As the building shakes, she moves with experience into a doorway and grips the jamb. Nevertheless, the vibrations are so intense that she is thrown to the floor. When the shaking stops, she will notice a man's legs, standing upright, outside her fourth-story window, as if he were floating in air. She will think that she is hallucinating. But the three floors below her no longer exist, and the collapsing building has carried her apartment to the sidewalk. (301)
>
> As the ground violently shakes and the sand boils of the Marina discharge materials from the liquefying depths, the things they spit up include tarpaper and bits of redwood—the charred remains of houses from the earthquake of 1906. (302)

In Golden Gate Park, high school girls are practicing field hockey. Their coach sees the playing field move, sees "huge trees . . . bending like windshield wipers." She thinks, This is the end, I'm about to fall into the earth, this is the way to go. Her players freeze in place. They are silent. They just look at one another. (293)

The final image that McPhee offers in *Assembling California* is one that accentuates humankind's precarious position on the shifting earth. He ends the story near Mussel Rock, where a man named Araullo is fishing with a long European pole for sea perch. The fisherman lives nearby, with an ocean view and a sense of fatalism. "'If it going to go down, it going to go down,' he shouted, and he flailed the green sea" (304). Like a character in a Robert Frost poem, Araullo cannot look out far or in deep; rather, he will take pleasure in his view of Mussel Rock, the cormorants and the pelicans, the shadow of a hang glider flickering over the "jumpy earth" (304) and dismiss the possibilities of deep time as he enjoys the present.

A Language to the Land

McPhee's geology quartet has proved difficult for some readers and dull for others. For many, though, the tetralogy is his most ambitious work. In an interview with Joan Hamilton, William Howarth discussed the overall achievement of the four books. "'He's lost some readers,' McPhee's colleague Howarth admits, 'but in time these books will be regarded as his masterwork. In four not-very-long books, he's helping us to see processes that are invisible. He's giving language to the land.'"[18] Perhaps Howarth's key phrase may be "in time," for the geology quartet, ultimately, seems to be about the nature of time. The final effect of the four volumes may be to place our often arrogant sense of time and our individual importance in the broader geological perspective, where human history is a blink in the history of the earth.

Tony Hillerman once said that he switched from journalism to fiction because he wanted to work with clay rather than marble, with something more malleable than hard facts. John McPhee has proven, specifically in his work on geology, that he can structure an inventive narrative out of the most ostensibly unyielding materials. In *Annals of the Former World,* he has taken on a subject as big as the planet and has made of it a story in which humanity is still a fascinating, if minor, character.

Chapter Eight
The Shape of the Future

McPhee's Achievement

John McPhee's twenty-three books to date represent an enormous achievement—one that is eclectic, consistent, and challenging. Those books—approximately one every year or so for the past thirty years—are an unwavering example of superb reporting and artful writing. Without ever compromising his allegiance to the authority of fact, McPhee is a subtly creative nonfiction artist. In his work, structure is always ingenious and sure. The sentences are invariably clear and informative, often gently humorous, sometimes sharply comic. His phrases often carry an epigrammatic energy reminiscent of Thoreau. His descriptions are striking and original. His grasp of scientific and technological matters is keen, and his depiction of his wilderness adventures seems dramatic and true. In a few syllables, at times comic and at others lyrical, he can characterize a subject or a scene—a professor with a "tenured waistline" (*Control,* 223), a naturalist with "Wedgewood-blue eyes" ("Keel," 143), a young man with "eyes that could make a driver's license shrivel and burn" ("Minihydro," 220). Describing the geologist David Love's testing of a rock by dripping hydrochloric acid on it, McPhee says, "the acid beaded up like an arching cat" (*Rising,* 193). In another story, he describes masonry "grouted with daylight" ("Minihydro," 208). In *The Crofter and the Laird,* he speaks of a group of women escaping from a cursing farmer "stilting along like scared blue herons" (67).

McPhee is a reporter, a man transported by facts, warmed by details, and in the careful attention to the specifics of a scene or a character's idiosyncrasies, he fashions stories cut from truth and made with art. It would be difficult to find a flaccid piece of phrasing or a careless bit of reporting in his voluminous work. What readers have noted are his clarity of mind, the generous sympathy of his artistic vision, his memorable characterizations, and his knack for finding the delicate balance between informing and dramatizing. His success as a writer comes first from his talent as a reporter. He is an artist who ventures into the world with a notebook in his hand. But without his openness to the world—be it a green market in New York City or a wilderness town in Alaska—he would have little chance of seeing with the fullness that he does.

A Spiritual Autobiography

On the surface, McPhee is one of the least self-referential of contemporary literary journalists, but in essence his books amount to a spiritual autobiography. Although his photograph has never appeared on any of his book jackets, over the course of his writing career, he has shown that he is more than the invisible journalist. In quiet bits and pieces in his books, he has revealed himself. He is left-handed and always carries a bandanna with him. He relishes good food and the company of interesting people. He takes pride in his Scottish heritage. He loves rivers, and his preferred mode of transportation is a canoe. Even the dedications in his books suggest the importance of family and friends to him. But it is between the lines that he reveals the most about himself. He spends time in the New Jersey Pine Barrens, on rivers in Maine, or in the back country of Alaska because it is a way to escape the congestion and sleeplessness of the urban world. Like Thoreau, McPhee has discovered that it is in the wilderness that he finds the kind of peace and the danger that bring life into focus. In *Oranges* McPhee suggests the salubrious effects of the natural world on him:

> The appeal of that world [the orange groves] and, to even a greater extent, the relief of it had increased in my mind with each day in the groves, among other reasons simply because gas stations, Burger Queens, and shopping centers so dominate the towns of central Florida that the over-all effect on a springtime visitor can be that he is in Trenton during an August heat wave. The groves, in absolute contrast, are both beautiful and quiet, at moments eerie. I retreated into them as often as I could. To someone who is alone in the groves, they can seem to be a vacant city, miles wide and miles long. (61–2)

There, in the groves, McPhee can enjoy the twilight, reading a book, lifted out of time. In his travels McPhee searches for places outside of time—the Jersey Pine Barrens, Colonsay, the Alaskan bush—places that have not been subsumed, Losangelized, and made into a replica of Trenton (which, for him, seems to symbolize a spiritless homogeneity).

McPhee's spiritual autobiography is implied in his choice of the places and the people that he writes about. All of his books, in this respect, have been a portrait of the artist, a picture of his motives, his values, his dreams and nightmares. His sketches of other people and the worlds they occupy hold up a mirror to his own face.[1] The traits he admires in the people he writes about—competence, a curiosity about the world around them, a moral perspective—are characteristics that define *him*. Like his characters, who are engaged deeply in some activity, McPhee is an expert craftsman, a writer who carves his narratives as precisely and meticulously as Henri Vaillancourt does his bark canoes.

Throughout McPhee's work, certain things communicate themselves unequivocally: his affection for nature; his belief in a meritocracy based upon skill; his affinity for people engaged in all manner of occupations, class and caste aside, as long as the individuals have a consuming interest in their vocations. In his stories McPhee seeks to describe not only a trustworthy and self-reliant American character but a specific sense of place. McPhee seems to search for harmony and balance in the world around him. Many of his books have been accounts of men and women struggling to find a sensible middle ground between the material needs of a technological society and the spiritual need for wilderness. Therefore, as a traveler and as a writer he has journeyed beyond the Trentons, away, it seems at times, from the modern world—into the beautifully anachronistic domain of Deerfield, the hardscrabble magnificence of Colonsay, the separateness of the Pine Barrens, Alaska, or northern Maine—in order to discover uncommon ground, where there is a chance that individuality can still be nurtured, the world's beauty preserved, and the earth's resources used wisely.

McPhee is a man of intellectual breadth, but he is also a writer who believes in the efficacy of experience. The characters in his stories— teachers, geologists, hunters, naturalists, artisans, doctors, seamen, farmers, engineers, and athletes—are all men and women of experience. Few of them are theoreticians. They are people who take knowledge from books or training and actively engage in work in the world, chipping away at rocks in a Nevada basin or smuggling illegal art from the former Soviet Union. They build dams, sail ships, care for patients, mine for gold, fight land developers. Similar to McPhee, they seem to take the word *education* to its root meaning, a leading out into the world.

All of McPhee's work leads his readers out into the world, emphasizing, as James Stull says, "the primacy of actual everyday experience." Stull goes on to say, "At times when the material world has for many readers lost its immediacy, and we live increasingly in a symbolically mediated, often hazily understood environment, McPhee's subjects make contact with and reaffirm a relation to the natural and immediate physical world. . . . Thus McPhee acts on the belief that knowledge is the provenance of all people."[2] McPhee's sympathetic imagination has a deeper, more novelistic turn than the skeptical consciousness of the investigative journalist. Generally, McPhee's object is to understand, not to criticize. His democratic instinct ("knowledge is the provenance of all people") leads him toward a structure and style that reflects the philosophical appropriateness of clear English and a discernible narrative design. McPhee celebrates individuality in person and location, and in each book he shapes a tale in which the people and places can speak through his prose style in a structure that seems true to the uniqueness of the story.

McPhee's Influence on a New Generation of Writers

It seems more than coincidence that John McPhee's work began in the 1960s at approximately the same time that the importance of creative nonfiction began to take root in the literary landscape. He is one of the seminal figures in the form, and a generation of recent writers of literary journalism owes him a debt for establishing many of the virtues and possibilities of the genre. Scholar and critic Norman Sims calls him "one of the most esteemed of the realists."[3] Tracy Kidder, who won the Pulitzer Prize for the nonfiction book *The Soul of a New Machine,* said, "McPhee has been my model. He's the most elegant of all the journalists writing today."[4] Lee Gutkind, the editor of the journal *Creative Nonfiction,* also sees McPhee as *the* model for younger writers who attempt to work within the form. "When anybody asks me what I do or what the journal does, I use the name of John McPhee and most people know immediately what this means. The kind of work that he has done—the impeccable quality of it—is the goal of writers in this genre. No other modern writer of nonfiction is more of a guidepost or beacon. McPhee supplied the vital element in this form of writing—the informational element. In the 1970s sometimes style served as the heart of certain renowned works of nonfiction. McPhee united style and substance and made the two of them together the foundation and anchor of the form."[5]

Walt Harrington, a writer for the *Washington Post* and the author of two books of nonfiction, says that McPhee influenced him as a writer in a number of ways. "First of all," Harrington says, "McPhee gave us the notion that if you got inside a topic, there was no boring subject." According to Harrington, when he was in graduate school, he read

McPhee's *Oranges* and was stunned into feeling, "My God, this man can make even oranges interesting." When Harrington read *A Sense of Where You Are,* he was impressed by McPhee's use of a simple idea to make a story cohere. Speaking of *Encounters with the Archdruid,* Harrington saw that McPhee "was not afraid, as many nonfiction writers seem to be, to set up a situation that would create a story." Harrington feels that this sort of intervention is fair territory for a nonfiction writer. "After all," Harrington commented, "this is not like a novelist plotting a story, but rather a journalist allowing a story line to emerge, to happen before the writer's eyes."[6]

Mark Singer, a staff writer for the *New Yorker* since the early 1970s when he had just graduated from college, said, "When I came here there was an intense awareness of McPhee and the kind of work he was doing." Singer feels that *Coming into the Country* forced everyone to notice McPhee's work but that he had begun to make his mark on the form long before that book. McPhee was one of the writers who helped make the genre legitimate. In Singer's words, "Of course, there is a tradition that McPhee is working in, but I think that the genre as a recognizable one wouldn't exist without him. McPhee always wanted to be a *New Yorker* writer, but he ended up re-inventing *New Yorker* journalism. Readers and critics were astonished by his prolificness. Academics were in awe of what he did—for he was able to do what they secretly hoped to do—take subjects that seemed uninteresting and make them fascinating." What readers like Singer sense about McPhee is that he is a brilliant man but not an arrogant one. McPhee's humanity comes through his careful prose, his eye for detail, his self-deprecating humor, his range of interests. Nonfiction writers like Singer studied McPhee's work because it has the quality of seamlessness, but they felt clearly the enormous amount of effort that went into producing each story. "McPhee showed us how to build a narrative in a truly artful way," Singer said. "For many of us, he remains the paragon of *New Yorker* journalism."[7]

Mike D'Orso, formerly a writer for the *Virginian-Pilot and Ledger-Star* and the author of six works of nonfiction, never studied journalism or writing formally. Instead, he learned from models, and early in his career his principal model was John McPhee. "*Coming into the Country* was my introduction to his writing," D'Orso said. "I read it with amazement. Everything was there—attention to detail, the right amount of research to put the reader into the story. . . . And for someone who cares so deeply about facts, as McPhee does, there was a weightlessness to his prose and a fluidity in his scenes. After *Coming into the Country,* I read everything he had written, and seeing his range emboldened me. He taught me that anything is fascinating if it is approached with fascination."[8]

In his introduction to *The Second John McPhee Reader,* David Remnick a former writing student of McPhee's at Princeton, suggests McPhee's widespread influence on nonfiction writers:

> More than half of his former students have gone on to work at various magazines and newspapers, to write books. Actually, only a small percentage of McPhee's students studied with him at Princeton; he has been for dozens and dozens of non-fiction writers what Robert Lowell used to be for poets and poet wannabes of a certain age: the model.
>
> To the degree that he revealed himself in the classroom, McPhee showed himself to be not unlike his first subject Bill Bradley—conservative about, and immersed in, the fundamentals of his craft. That is, he is conservative, blessedly conservative, when it comes to fact. His principle is that non-fiction can, and should, borrow the varied structures of fiction, but not its license.[9]

As Remnick understands, McPhee has taught a generation of younger writers that the creation of intricate scenes, the use of a literary style, and the ethics of good journalism are not incompatible.

Mark Kramer, writer in residence at Boston University and author of a number of highly regarded nonfiction books, feels that McPhee's influence on his own writing was significant:

> I read *The Headmaster* early on, and *Oranges* while I was writing about farming. I knew that I was interested in non-fiction because even in my twenties, I wanted to know how institutions and organizations really worked. Newspaper feature stories, I sensed, forced me to reach in and discover in them details that hinted at personality, power, real economic issues, real emotions, the quirky ways people say things. There are good reasons newspapers describe a version of reality as they do, but it never seemed complete, and rarely seemed essential to me.
>
> And there was John McPhee. It was as if a friend with the same turn and intensity of personal interest in his topics had gone there and was describing what really went on over supper, in a chat that took my full knowledge and comprehension of how the world worked into account. It's the aspect of literary journalism that I call the intimate voice. McPhee dealt with the complexities of his people and topics at what Henry James calls the "felt life" level. It contradicted official versions of things without seeming rebellious or contentiously political. It was simply McPhee, autonomous writer.

He has continued to impress me with his audacious, playful structures and voice, which is poised and independent, but affectionate toward most of his subjects. McPhee was sure-footed enough to comprehend the possibility of turning the world's slowest narrative subject—the grinding down of rocks—into an exciting narrative. He was a writer's writer when I started writing seriously in 1978, and he still is that.[10]

Clearly, McPhee's work has influenced a new generation of creative nonfiction writers. More important, perhaps, he has reached his readers—and this has been his goal all along. "I hope that there is a chance," he said, "that my books will be read for a while. Carving out these things over the years, I have had the same goal each and every time: to make something that stands on its own feet. And I always have the same hope, that it will not come unstuck immediately. I am pleased, for instance, that young people still read *A Sense of Where You Are* and write to me about it. I want to write books that are absorbing to read: there is no message in them but that."[11]

The message at the heart of his work—the message that can be found in the humility and the humanity of the writer, through his dedication to accuracy, his sensitivity to the nuances of character, his attention to the complexities of structure—is that he is a storyteller of the first rank, an artist whose gift is in the shaping of fact into enduring narrative.

Notes and References

Preface

1. Donald McQuade et al., eds., *The Harper American Literature,* vol. 2 (New York: Harper and Row, 1987), 2601.

Chapter One

1. William Howarth, Introduction to *The John McPhee Reader* (New York: Farrar, Straus and Giroux, 1976), ix.
2. John McPhee, in interviews with Michael Pearson on five occasions from the fall of 1992 to the summer of 1995. Future references will be cited parenthetically as Personal Interview.
3. John McPhee, *The Crofter and the Laird* (New York: Farrar, Straus and Giroux, 1970), 9. Future references to McPhee's work will be cited parenthetically in the text.
4. Norman Sims, "John McPhee," in *American Writers* (New York: Charles Scribner's Sons, 1991), 290.
5. Howarth, "Introduction," ix.
6. Alfred Hare, Jr., interview with Michael Pearson, 23 August 1995.
7. John McPhee, letter to Alfred Hare, Jr., 9 August 1972.
8. Sims, "John McPhee," 295.
9. John McPhee, "Eucalyptus Trees," *The Reporter,* 19 October 1967, 36–9.
10. John McPhee, "Ruth, the Sun is Shining," *Playboy,* April 1968, 114.
11. John McPhee in Douglas Vipond and Russell A. Hunt's "The Strange Case of the Queen-Post Truss: John McPhee on Writing and Reading," *College Composition and Communications* 42, no. 2 (May 1991): 207.
12. Pamela Marsh, "The Lively Snippet, the Appetizing Trifle," *Christian Science Monitor,* 1 February 1969, 9.
13. Howarth, "Introduction," xi.
14. Ronald Weber, *The Literature of Fact* (Athens: Ohio University Press, 1980), 121.

Chapter Two

1. Theodore A. Rees Cheney, *Writing Creative Nonfiction* (Berkeley, CA: Ten Speed Press, 1991), 1.
2. Weber, *The Literature of Fact,* 33–41. In chapter 5, "Zero Interpretation," Weber discusses the speculation about the current appeal of nonfiction.

3. Joseph M. Webb, "Historical Perspective on the New Journalism," *Journalism History* (Summer 1974): 40.

4. Louis Landa, Introduction to *A Journal of the Plague Year* by Daniel Defoe (London: Oxford University Press, 1969), xxxix.

5. Howarth, Introduction, vii.

6. John Hellman, *Fables of Fact: The New Journalism as New Fiction* (Urbana: University of Illinois Press, 1981), 1.

7. David Lodge, *The Novelist at the Crossroads* (Ithaca, NY: Cornell University Press, 1971), 33.

8. Mas'ud Zavarzadeh, quoted in Phyllis Frus, *The Politics and Poetics of Journalistic Narrative: The Timely and the Timeless* (Cambridge: Cambridge University Press, 1994), 56.

9. Chris Anderson, *Style as Argument: Contemporary American Nonfiction* (Carbondale: Southern Illinois University Press, 1987), 2.

10. Thomas B. Connery, "A Third Way to Tell the Story: American Literary Journalism at the Turn of the Century," in *Literary Journalism in the Twentieth Century,* ed. Norman Sims (New York and Oxford: Oxford University Press, 1990), 3–7.

11. W. Ross Winterowd, *The Rhetoric of the "Other" Literature* (Carbondale: Southern Illinois University Press, 1990).

12. Barbara Lounsberry, *The Art of Fact: Contemporary Artists of Nonfiction* (Westport, CT: Greenwood Press, 1990), xi.

13. Ibid., xiii–xviii.

14. Tom Wolfe, Introduction to *The New Journalism,* ed. Tom Wolfe (New York: Harper and Row, 1973), 3–36.

15. Gay Talese, an interview with John Brady, reprinted in Ronald Weber, *The Reporter as Artist: A Look at the New Journalism Controversy* (New York: Hastings House, 1974), 110.

16. Norman Sims, *The Literary Journalists* (New York: Ballantine Books, 1984), 3–25.

17. See "The Art of Literary Journalism" and "Breakable Rules for Literary Journalists," in *Literary Journalism: A New Collection of the Best American Nonfiction,* ed. Norman Sims and Mark Kramer (New York: Ballantine Books, 1995), 3–34.

18. Sims, "The Art of Literary Journalism," 3.

19. Susan Orlean and Tracy Kidder are both quoted in Sims, "The Art of Literary Nonfiction," 4 and 19.

20. Kramer, "Breakable Rules for Literary Journalists," 34.

21. Joseph Mitchell, quoted in Norman Sims, "Joseph Mitchell and The New Yorker Nonfiction Writers," in *Literary Journalism in the Twentieth Century,* ed. Norman Sims (New York and Oxford: Oxford University Press, 1990), 99.

22. Hugh Kenner, "The Politics of the Plain Style," in *Literary Journalism in the Twentieth Century,* ed. Norman Sims (New York and Oxford: Oxford University Press, 1990), 187.

23. Thomas Kunkel, *Genius in Disguise: Harold Ross of "The New Yorker"* (New York: Random House, 1995), 301.

24. Willie Morris, *New York Days* (Boston: Little, Brown and Company, 1993), 17.

25. Rex Lardner, "Shoot That Ball!" *New York Times Book Review,* 28 November 1965, 71.

26. Howarth, Introduction, vii.

27. Joan Hamilton, "An Encounter with John McPhee," *Sierra* (May–June 1990): 52.

28. Kathy Smith, "John McPhee Balances the Act," in *Literary Journalism in the Twentieth Century,* ed. Norman Sims (New York and Oxford: Oxford University Press, 1990), 205.

29. David Remnick, "Notes from Underground," *New York Review of Books,* 2 March 1995, 11.

30. Robert Coles, "Alaska, the State that Came in from the Cold," *Book World—The Washington Post,* 22 January 1978, F1.

31. Remnick, "Notes from Underground," 11.

32. Weber, *The Literature of Fact,* 116.

Chapter Three

1. James N. Stull, "Self and the Performance of Others: The Pastoral Vision of John McPhee," in *Literary Selves: Autobiography and Contemporary American Nonfiction* (Westport, CT: Greenwood Press, 1993), 15.

2. Lounsberry, *The Art of Fact,* 65–106.

3. Stull, "Self and the Performance of Others," 7.

4. David Remnick, "Notes from Underground," 11. Remnick uses this phrase to describe what McPhee *is not.*

5. Ibid.

6. Mark Kramer, quoted in *The Literary Journalist,* 11.

7. David Brower, quoted in Hamilton, "An Encounter with John McPhee," 53.

8. McPhee, quoted in *The Literary Journalist,* 9.

9. Sandra Schmidt Oddo, "How to Not Make an Atomic Bomb," *New York Times Book Review,* 23 June 1974, 4.

10. Smith, "John McPhee Balances the Act," 215.

11. Winterowd, *The Rhetoric of the "Other" Literature,* 79.

12. Lounsberry, *The Art of Fact,* 67.

13. Ibid., 74.

14. John McPhee, quoted in Jared Haynes, "The Size and Shape of the Canvas: An Interview with John McPhee," *Writing on the Edge* 5, no. 2 (Spring 1994): 113–4.

15. Howarth, Introduction, xii–xvii.

16. McPhee, quoted in Haynes, "The Size and Shape of the Canvas," 109.

17. Ibid., 114.

Chapter Four

  1. Kunkel, *Genius in Disguise,* see 105–8 and 301–3.
  2. John McPhee, untitled essay, *New Yorker,* 28 December 1992, 137.
  3. John McPhee, quoted in Sims, "John McPhee," 296.
  4. Lounsberry, *The Art of Fact,* 66.
  5. Ibid., 67.
  6. John McPhee, quoted in Sims, *The Literary Journalists,* 24.
  7. Remnick, "Notes from Underground," 10.
  8. Ibid.
  9. Lounsberry, *The Art of Fact,* 68–9.
 10. Sims, "John McPhee," 294.
 11. Smith, "John McPhee Balances the Act," 212.
 12. Edward Hoagland, "From John McPhee with Love and Craftsman-ship," *New York Times Book Review,* 22 June 1975, 3.
 13. McPhee quoted in Dennis Drabelle, "A Conversation with John McPhee," *Sierra* (October–December 1978): 63.
 14. Howarth, Introduction to *The Headmaster,* 23.
 15. See Roderick Cook, *Harper's* (March 1967): 139. Also see an un-signed review in the *New York Times Book Review,* 26 February 1967, 45.
 16. See Sims, *The Literary Journalists,* 14. Also see Howarth, *The John McPhee Reader,* 81.
 17. For a full discussion of this issue see Haynes, "The Size and Shape of the Canvas," 123.
 18. McPhee, quoted in Haynes, "The Size and Shape of the Canvas," 123.
 19. Ibid., 123–4.
 20. Ibid., 116.
 21. Ibid.
 22. Hoagland, "From John McPhee with Love and Craftsmanship," 3.
 23. Howarth, *The John McPhee Reader,* 267.
 24. McPhee, quoted in Haynes, "The Size and Shape of the Canvas," 113–4.
 25. Remnick, "Notes From Underground," 11.
 26. See Harlow Robinson, "He Who Smuggles Must Learn to Party," *New York Times Book Review,* 18 December 1994, 24.
 27. Stull, "Self and the Performance of Others," 15.

Chapter Five

  1. Eric J. Leed, *The Mind of the Traveler: From Gilgamesh to Global Tourism* (New York: Basic Books, 1991), 105.
  2. Ibid., 287.

3. Howarth, *The John McPhee Reader*, 53.
4. Hoagland, *New York Times Book Review*, 22 June 1975, 26.
5. James Kaufmann, *The Christian Science Monitor*, 18 May 1984, 18.
6. Edward Hoagland, "Where Life Begins Over," *New York Times Book Review*, 27 November 1977, 48.
7. It is interesting to note that McPhee draws analogies between Alaska and Scotland approximately half a dozen times in *Coming into the Country*.
8. Weber, *The Literature of Fact*, 117.
9. Ernest Hemingway, "Indian Camp," *The Short Stories* (New York: Collier Books, 1986), 95.
10. John McPhee, Appendix to "Skimmer Burns," unpublished thesis (Princeton University, 1953), 259.
11. Weber, *The Literature of Fact*, 119.
12. Lounsberry, *The Art of Fact*, 81.

Chapter Six

1. John Skow, "Bombs in Gilead?" *Time*, 10 June 1974, 94.
2. Sandra Schmidt Oddo, "How to Not Make an Atomic Bomb," *New York Times Book Review*, 23 June 1974, 4.
3. Barbara Lounsberry, "John McPhee's Levels of the Earth," in *The Art of Fact: Contemporary Artists of Nonfiction* (Westport, CT: Greenwood Press, 1990), 70, 74.
4. Steven Millhauser, *Edwin Mullhouse: The Life and Death of an American Writer 1943–1954 by Jeffrey Cartwright* (New York: Alfred A. Knopf, 1972), 75.
5. Lounsberry, "John McPhee's Levels of the Earth," 73.
6. Hamilton, "An Encounter with John McPhee," 53.
7. McPhee, quoted in Michael Pearson, *A Place That's Known* (Jackson: University Press of Mississippi, 1994), 154.
8. Lounsberry, "John McPhee's Levels of the Earth," 105. She points out that the Aeron group disbands and another circle in one of McPhee's works contracts.

Chapter Seven

1. Hamilton, "An Encounter with John McPhee," 54.
2. McPhee tells the entire story of the genesis of *The Control of Nature* in Haynes, "The Size and Shape of the Canvas," 120.
3. McPhee quoted in Haynes, "The Size and Shape of the Canvas" (part I), 114.
4. Stephen Jay Gould, "Deep Time and Creaseless Motion," *New York Review of Books*, 14 May 1981, 26–7.
5. Robert D. Hatcher, "Layers of Time," *Natural History* (April 1983): 93.
6. Beaufort Cranford, "Quills in the Hills," *Detroit News*, 13 May 1984, 2M.

7. Amy Meeker, "Short Reviews," *Atlantic* (May 1981): 82.

8. Michiko Kakutani, "The Writing in the Rocks," *New York Times Book Review*, 30 January 1993, 1.

9. Winterowd, *The Rhetoric of the "Other" Literature*, 83.

10. Lounsberry, *The Art of Fact*, 96.

11. Paul Zweig, "Rhapsodist of Deep Time," *New York Times Book Review*, 17 May 1981, 1, 33.

12. Ibid., 33.

13. Lounsberry, *The Art of Fact*, 97.

14. See McPhee's interview with Jared Haynes, "The Size and Shape of the Canvas" (part II), 114–5.

15. Evan S. Connell, "Snapshot of a Billion Years," *New York Times Book Review*, 23 November 1986, 15.

16. Gretel Ehrlich, *The Solace of Open Spaces* (New York: Viking Penguin, 1985), 15.

17. Lounsberry, *The Art of Fact*, 100.

18. Howarth, quoted in Hamilton, "An Encounter with John McPhee," 92.

Chapter Eight

1. Appropriately, it seems, McPhee is now beginning to work on a book about his writing methods and his intentions, a sort of autobiography of the artist's mind.

2. Stull, "Self and the Performance of Others," 28.

3. Norman Sims, ed., *Literary Journalism in the Twentieth Century* (New York and Oxford: Oxford University Press, 1990), viii.

4. Kidder quoted in Sims, *The Literary Journalists* (New York: Ballantine, 1984), 163.

5. Personal interview with Lee Gutkind, December 1995.

6. Personal interview with Walt Harrington, November 1995.

7. Personal interview with Mark Singer, November 1995.

8. Personal interview with Mike D'Orso, December 1995.

9. David Remnick, Introduction to *The Second John McPhee Reader*, ed. Patricia Strachan (New York: Farrar, Straus and Giroux, 1996), x.

10. Personal interview with Mark Kramer, December 1995.

11. Personal interview with John McPhee, December 1995.

Selected Bibliography

PRIMARY SOURCES

Books

(All published by Farrar, Straus and Giroux [New York].)
Assembling California, 1993.
Basin and Range, 1981.
Coming into the Country, 1977.
The Control of Nature, 1989.
The Crofter and the Laird, 1970.
The Curve of Binding Energy, 1974.
The Deltoid Pumpkin Seed, 1973.
Encounters with the Archdruid, 1971.
Giving Good Weight, 1979.
The Headmaster, 1966.
Levels of the Game, 1969.
Looking for a Ship, 1990.
Oranges, 1967.
Pieces of the Frame, 1975.
The Pine Barrens, 1968.
La Place de la Concorde Suisse, 1984.
The Ransom of Russian Art, 1994.
Rising from the Plains, 1986.
A Roomful of Hovings and Other Profiles, 1968.
A Sense of Where You Are, 1965.
The Survival of the Bark Canoe, 1975.
In Suspect Terrain, 1983.
Table of Contents, 1985.

Selected Uncollected Stories and Essays

Fiction:

"The Fair of San Gennaro." *The TransAtlantic Review* 8 (Winter 1961):117–28.
"Eucalyptus Trees." *The Reporter,* 19 October 1967, 36–9.
"Ruth, the Sun Is Shining." *Playboy* (April 1968):114–6, 126, 186.

Nonfiction from the New Yorker:

"Travels of the Rock," 26 February 1990, 108–17.
"Irons in the Fire," 20 December 1993, 94–113.

The Talk of the Town articles in the New Yorker:

"Big Plane," 19 February 1966, 28.
"Two Commissioners" (Thomas Hoving), 5 March 1966, 33.
"Coliseum Hour," 12 March 1966, 44.
"Beauty and Horror," 28 May 1966, 28.
"Girl in a Paper Dress," 25 June 1966, 20.
"On the Way to Gladstone," 9 July 1966, 17.
"Ms and FeMs at the Biltmore," 12 July 1966.
"The License Plates of Burning Tree," 30 January 1971, 20.
"Three Gatherings" (Americans), 25 December 1971, 25.
"The Conching Rooms," 13 May 1972, 32.
"Sullen Gold," 25 March 1974, 32.
"Flavors & Fragrances," 8 April 1974, 35.
"Police Story," 15 July 1974, 27.
" 'Time' Covers, NR," 28 October 1974, 40.
"The P-1800," 10 February 1975, 30.
"In Virgin Forest," 6 July 1987, 21–3.
"Release," 28 September 1987, 28–32.
"Altimeter Man," 25 September 1989, 48–50.

Articles in Time *and selected magazines:*

Time cover stories on Mort Sahl (15 August 1960), Jean Kerr (14 April 1961), Jackie Gleason (29 December 1961), Sophia Loren (6 April 1962), Joan Baez (23 November 1962), Richard Burton (26 April 1963), Barbra Streisand (10 April 1964), the New York World's Fair (5 June 1964).
". . . Josie's Well." *Holiday* (January 1970):66+.
"Pieces of the Frame." *The Atlantic* (January 1970):42–7.
"Centre Court." *Playboy* (June 1971):102+.
"Tennis." *New York Times Book Review,* 10 June 1973, 1+.
"The People of New Jersey's Pine Barrens." *National Geographic* 145 (January 1974):52–77. Pictures by W. R. Curtsinger.

Unpublished Work

Skimmer Burns, a novel presented as a senior thesis at Princeton University, 1953.

SECONDARY SOURCES
Books and Articles

Brown, Spencer. "The Odor of Durability." *Sewanee Review* (Winter 1978): 146–52. Compares and contrasts the work of E. B. White and John McPhee, as he says, "two of our foremost essayists."

Clark, Joanne K. "The Writings of John Angus McPhee: A Selected Bibliography." *Bulletin of Bibliography* (January–March 1981):45–51. Good source on work he produced up until 1981. But there have been eight books since then.

Eason, David. "The New Journalism and the Image-World." In *Literary Journalism in the Twentieth Century*, ed. Norman Sims, 191–205. New York: Oxford University Press, 1990. Eason makes a distinction between nonfiction writers who are realists, such as Tom Wolfe and Gay Talese, and those who are modernists, such as Joan Didion and Norman Mailer. The dominant function of a realist report, Eason says, is to reveal an interpretation. For a modernist, it is to demonstrate how an interpretation is constructed.

Espey, David. "The Wilds of New Jersey: John McPhee as Travel Writer." In *Temperamental Journeys: Essays on the Modern Literature of Travel*, ed. Michael Kowalewski, 164–75. Athens: University of Georgia Press, 1992. Espey compares McPhee to Thoreau as a travel writer who places serious emphasis on the study of nature, rejecting travel as "merely a leisure dimension." In his travels, Espey says, McPhee studies not only the natural world but the disciplines and the characters of his guides.

Hamilton, Joan. "An Encounter with John McPhee." *Sierra* (May–June 1990):50–5, 92, 96. Hamilton's article is an interview/profile that focuses upon McPhee's nature writing. She emphasizes McPhee's narrative skills and his "staunch openness" in approaching his subjects. Hamilton delves into McPhee's methodology and his fascination with narrative structure.

Howarth, William. Introduction to *The John McPhee Reader*, vii–xxiii. New York: Farrar, Straus and Giroux, 1976. This remains the definitive account of McPhee's methods and motives. It also offers a superb introduction to his life. In addition there are sharp insights about the themes that run throughout his books. Any study of McPhee should begin with this essay.

Lounsberry, Barbara. "John McPhee's Levels of the Earth." In *The Art of Fact: Contemporary Artists of Nonfiction*, 65–106. Westport, CT: Greenwood Press, 1990. Lounsberry examines the relationship between structure and theme in McPhee's work, focusing particularly on the image of the circle and how it appears in his various books. Lounsberry makes brilliant connections between McPhee's images of circles and levels and shows convincingly how they relate to the representative men and women he profiles. She places McPhee's work within the tradition of Emerson and Thoreau and says that his books amount to a "twentieth-century tempering of Thoreau's and Emerson's relentless idealism."

Remnick, David. "Notes from Underground." *New York Review of Books*, 2 March 1995, 10–3. A brilliant, if not unbiased, interpretation of

McPhee's achievement by one of his former students and a current *New Yorker* staff writer.

————. Introduction to *The Second John McPhee Reader*, ed. Patricia Strochan. New York: Farrar, Straus and Giroux, 1996. Slightly modified and expanded version of Remnick's essay from the *New York Review of Books*.

Sims, Norman. "The Literary Journalists." Introduction to *The Literary Journalists*, 3–25. New York: Ballantine, 1984. Through interviews with literary journalists such as Mark Singer and Tracy Kidder, Sims points out the essential elements of the form—immersion reporting, complex structure, accuracy, voice, ethical responsibility, and symbolic realities. It is a practical and intelligent summary of the basic aspects of the genre.

————, ed. *Literary Journalism in the Twentieth Century*. New York and Oxford: Oxford University Press, 1990. A collection of essays by scholars on a variety of literary journalists, past and present.

————. "John McPhee." In *American Writers*, 289–315. New York: Charles Scribners' Sons, 1991. A general survey of McPhee's life and works.

————. "The Art of Literary Journalism." In *Literary Journalism: A New Collection of the Best American Nonfiction*, ed. Norman Sims and Mark Kramer, 3–34. New York: Ballantine Books, 1995. An update of Sims's essay in *The Literary Journalists*. He speaks with a few different writers and expands or modifies some of his previous ideas. See also Mark Kramer's "Breakable Rules for Literary Journalists" in the same volume. Kramer's essay is based upon his own experience as a writer of creative nonfiction.

Smith, Kathy. "John McPhee Balances the Act." In *Literary Journalism in the Twentieth Century*, ed. Norman Sims, 206–27. New York: Oxford University Press, 1990. Smith looks at McPhee's work through the lens of contemporary literary theory. From her perspective McPhee carefully structures each of his narratives to create meaning. As her argument develops, she says that all representation depends upon artifice and therefore McPhee clearly "fashions" the truth rather than reports it. She refers to McPhee's nonfiction as a "fictionalizing act, whether he acknowledges it or not."

Stull, James N. "Self and the Performance of Others: The Pastoral Vision of John McPhee." In *Literary Selves: Autobiography and Contemporary American Nonfiction*, 11–28. Westport, CT: Greenwood Press, 1993. This essay offers a cogent analysis of some of the central themes in McPhee's work. In particular, Stull focuses on the pastoral vision at the heart of McPhee's narratives and the prototypical McPhee hero—"competent, trustworthy, and morally good." Stull agrees with Kathy Smith's thesis in "John McPhee Balances the Act," and he feels that McPhee's nonfiction "transcends realistic portraiture . . . and creates a gallery of heroic selves within the context of everyday experience."

Vipond, Douglas and Russell A. Hunt. "The Strange Case of the Queen-Post Truss: John McPhee on Writing and Reading." *College Composition and*

Communication 42, no. 2 (May 1991):200–10. Vipond and Hunt conduct a discourse-based interview with McPhee in which they focus, with the writer, on specific passages from his books. The interviewers change certain words or sentences in the passage, present them to the writer, and they ask why he would or would not be willing to change the text. In the process of the exchange, McPhee offers some valuable insights about his writing process.

Weber, Ronald. "Letting Subjects Grow: Literary Nonfiction from the *New Yorker.*" *Antioch Review* (Fall 1978):486–99. Reprinted in Ronald Weber. *The Literature of Fact: Literary Nonfiction in American Writing,* 111–22. Athens: Ohio University Press, 1980. For a general overview of literary nonfiction, Weber's book is excellent. The chapter on McPhee restricts itself to a discussion of *Coming into the Country.* Weber argues that *Coming into the Country* is art because it gives weight and significance to the particular and endows the particular with resonant meanings.

Winterowd, Ross W. "John McPhee and the Craft of Writing." In *The Rhetoric of the "Other" Literature,* 79–83. Carbondale: Southern Illinois University Press, 1990. Winterowd's thesis is that McPhee is able to use structure to convey facts and judgments. To make his point, Winterowd examines *Rising from the Plains* as an example of McPhee's rhetorical strategies.

Selected Interviews

Drabble, Dennis. "Conversations with John McPhee." *Sierra* (October–December 1978):61–3.

Haynes, Jared. "The Size and Shape of the Canvas: An Interview with John McPhee." *Writing on the Edge* 5, no. 2 (Spring 1994):109–25; and 6, no. 1 (Fall 1994):108–25.

Pearson, Michael. "Twenty Questions: A Conversation with John McPhee." *Creative Nonfiction* (Fall 1993):76–87.

Index

Addison, Joseph, 12
Agee, James, 15; *Let Us Now Praise Famous Men,* 16
Anderson, Chris, 13
Armies of the Night, 17, 70
Ashe, Arthur, 25, 28, 43–46
Augustine, *Confessions,* 12

Boone, Daniel, 81
Baez, Joan, 8
Barth, John, 11, 17
Barthelme, Donald, 11, 17
Bellow, Saul, 20, 63
Borges, Jorge Luis, 11
Boswell, James, 12
Boyden, Frank L., 3, 23, 24, 27, 36–38, 39, 43, 50, 57
Boyden, Helen, 3
Bradley, Bill, 9, 23, 24, 27, 33–36, 37, 39, 40, 43, 50, 56, 57, 60
Brautigan, Richard, 17
Brower, David, 24, 46–49, 55, 100, 101, 117
Brown, Fred, 62–65
Browning, Robert, 57
Burton, Richard, 8

Camus, Albert, 63
Candler, Sam, 24, 51–53
Canterbury Tales, The, 12
Capek, Carl, 93
Capote, Truman, 11, 13, 16, 17
Carter, Jimmy, 51, 53
Casteneda, Pedro de, 12
Chase, Andy, 49–51
Chatwin, Bruce, 12
Cheney, Theodore Rees, 11
Coles, Robert, 19
Columbus, Christopher, 49, 87
Connell, Evan S., 115
Connery, Thomas, 13
Cook, Dick, 80–81, 100
Coover, Robert, 17

Copernicus, 87
Crane, Stephen, 16
Cranford, Beaufort, 109
Crockett, Davy, 65, 81

Darwin, Charles, 112
Deffeyes, Kenneth, 110, 112, 117
Defoe, Daniel, 12
Didion, Joan, 11, 17
Dillard, Annie, 18, 116
Dodge, Norton, 57–60
Dominy, Floyd, 47–49, 101
D'Orso, Mike, 126–27
Drew, Monroe, 94–97
Dyson, Freeman, 87, 88

Eckert, Richard, 91–92
Ehrlich, Gretel, 18, 116
Einstein, Albert, 87
Eliot, George, 15
Emerson, Ralph Waldo, 12, 21, 36, 59
Esquire, 8

Faulkner, William, 87
Fielding, Joseph, 12
Franklin, Benjamin, 21
Fraser, Charles, 47–48
Frazier, Ian, 12, 19
Frost, Robert, 78, 121

Gaugin, Paul, 77
Gelvins (Ed and Stanley), 82–83, 93
Genofile, Bob, 106–108
Gibbons, Euell, 40–41, 43, 60
Gleason, Jackie, 8
Gould, Stephen Jay, 109
Graduate, The, 70
Graebner, Clark, 25, 28, 43–46
Grapes of Wrath, The, 38
Gutkind, Lee, 125

Hakluyt, Richard, 12
Hamilton, Joan, 19, 90, 102, 121
Hare, Alfred, Jr., 5

141

Harper's, 17, 38
Harrington, Walt, 125–26
Harris, Anita, 110, 113–14
Hawthorne, Nathaniel, 55
Hellman, John, 13
Hemingway, Ernest, 78
Herr, Michael, *Dispatches,* 17
Hersey, John, *Hiroshima,* 15, 16
Hillerman, Tony, 121
Hoagland, Edward, 37, 51, 67, 73
Homer, 73
Hornsby, Rogers, 49
Hoving, Thomas, 24, 39–40, 43, 50, 57
Howard, Euan, 69
Howarth, William, 1, 4, 9, 13, 18, 19,
    29–30, 38, 52, 64, 121
Hunt, Russell, 7
Hutton, James, 112

Irving, Washington, 12, 63

James, Henry, 23, 127
Joyce, James, 16

Kakutani, Michiko, 109–110
Kauffmann, John, 101
Kenner, Hugh, 15, 24
Kidder, Tracy, 15, 125
Kleinspehn, Karen, 110–11
Kramer, Mark, 15, 127–28
Kukon, John, 96–98
Kunkel, Thomas, 32

Landa, Louis, 12
Lardner, Rex, 18
Lardner, Ring, 8
Least Heat-Moon, William, 12, 18
Lee, Robert E., 37
Leed, Eric J., 62–63
Lieb, Alan, 24, 42–43
Liebling, A.J., 16, 32
Literary nonfiction, 5, 10, 11–20; features
    of, 13–15, 23–31
Lodge, David, 13
Loren, Sophia, 8
Lounsberry, Barbara, 13, 14, 21, 27, 33,
    36, 80, 86, 90, 110, 111, 113, 117

Love, David, 110, 111, 114–17
Luther, Martin, 113

McGlynn, Robert, 3, 6
McGuiness, James, 32
McKee, Olive, 3, 4, 6, 29
McKelway, St. Clair, 32
McNeill, Donald, 69
McPhee, John; study at Cambridge, 1, 4,
    5, 8, 9; Deerfield Academy, 1, 3, 4, 6;
    early life, 1–6; Keewaydin Camp,
    4–5, 21, 22, 96, 110; the McPhee
    hero, 1, 3, 32–61; *Nassau Literary
    Magazine,* 4; *Nassau Sovereign,* 4; *New
    York Times Magazine,* 4; pastoral
    images in his work, 21–22; Princeton
    (town and university), 1, 2–4, 5, 21,
    22, 30, 33, 62, 63, 64, 96; *Princeton
    Alumni Weekly,* 4; *Princeton Tyger,* 4;
    work for "Robert Montgomery Pre-
    sents," 8; sense of place in his writing,
    62–84; *Time* magazine, 4, 8, 33;
    "Twenty Questions" (radio and televi-
    sion show), 4, 6; writing methods,
    29–31

BOOKS
*Annals of the Former World (Basin and
    Range, In Suspect Terrain, Rising
    from the Plains,* and *Assembling Cali-
    fornia),* 108–121, 122
Coming into the Country, 19, 22, 23,
    27–28, 73–84, 93, 126
Control of Nature, The, 103–108, 122
Crofter and the Laird, The, 62, 68–71,
    122
Curve of Binding Energy, The, 85–91
Deltoid Pumpkin Seed, The, 92, 94–99
Encounters with the Archdruid, 5, 22,
    27, 28, 46–49, 55, 126
Giving Good Weight, 42, 91, 100
Headmaster, The, 3, 24, 36–38, 127
John McPhee Reader, The, 1, 13, 29
Levels of the Game, 25, 27, 28, 43–46,
    49
Looking for a Ship, 49–51
Oranges, 38–39, 126, 127
Pieces of the Frame, 51, 67

Pine Barrens, The, 5, 22, 23, 24–25,
     62–67, 68, 71, 96
Place de la Concorde Suisse, La, 71–73
Ransom of Russian Art, The, 57–60
Roomful of Hovings, A, 39–40
Sense of Where You Are, A, 9, 18,
     33–36, 58, 126, 128
Second John McPhee Reader, The, 127
Survival of the Bark Canoe, The, 28–29,
     52–57
Table of Contents, 60, 93

ESSAYS AND STORIES
"Atlantic Generating Station, The,"
     91–93
"Basketball and Beefeaters," 4, 6, 8
"Brigade de Cuisine," 41–43
"Eucalyptus Trees," 7
"Forager, A," 40–41
"Heirs of General Practice," 53
"Keel of Lake Dickey, The,"
     100–103, 122
"Minihydro," 93–94, 122
"North of the C.P. Line," 60–61
"Open Man," 53
"Ruth, the Sun is Shining," 7
"Search for Marvin Gardens, The,"
     67–68
"Travels in Georgia," 23, 51–53

UNPUBLISHED WORK
Skimmer Burns, 4, 6, 7

McPhee, Angus, 2
McPhee, Harry Roemer, 2, 9, 33
McPhee, Jenny, 9
McPhee, Laura, 9
McPhee, Laura Anne, 2
McPhee, Martha, 9
McPhee, Mary Ziegler, 2
McPhee, Roemer, 2
McPhee, Sarah, 9
McPhee, Yolanda, 9
Mailer, Norman, 11, 17
Marsh, Pamela, 8
Meeker, Amy, 109
Melville, Hermann, 12; *Moby Dick,* 51
Miller, William, 94–97, 99

Millhauser, Steven, 86
Mitchell, Joseph, *Joe Gould's Secret,* 15, 16,
     18, 32
Moores, Eldridge, 110, 117–20
Morris, Willie, 17
Muir, John, 115

New Journalism, The, 14
New Yorker, 4, 6, 8, 9, 16, 17, 19, 32, 33,
     38, 126

O'Connor, Flannery, 81
Oddo, Sandra Schmidt, 26, 86
Orlean, Susan, 15
Orwell, George, *Down and Out in Paris
     and London, Homage to Catalonia,* and
     Road to Wigan Pier, The, 16

Park, Charles, 46–47
Percy, Walker, 103
Preston, Richard, 18
Pynchon, Thomas, 17

Remnick, David, 19, 22, 35, 36, 58,
     127
Rhodes, Richard, 14
Richardson, Samuel, 12
Ross, Harold, 32
Ruckdeschel, Carol, 23, 51–53, 80

Sands, General Thomas, 104–105
Shakespeare, William, 115
Shawn, William, 32–33
Sims, Norman, 5, 14, 15, 33, 34, 37, 39,
     125
Singer, Mark, 18, 126; *Mr. Personality,* 19
Skow, John, 85
Smith, Herbert, 67
Smith, John, 12, 65
Smith, Kathy, 19, 26, 37
Steele, Richard, 12
Streisand, Barbra, 8
Stull, James N., 21, 22, 59, 124–25

Talese, Gay, 11, 12, 14; *Honor Thy Father*
     and *Kingdom and the Power, The,* 17
Taylor, Ted, 85–91, 96, 116, 117
Thompson, Hunter S., 18

Thoreau, Henry David, 12, 15, 18, 21, 51, 52, 56, 59, 80, 115, 122, 123
Twain, Mark, 12, 22, 62, 105

Ulam, Stanislaw, 87

Vaillancourt, Henri, 28–29, 53–57, 60, 81, 96, 124
Verne, Jules, 87, 88
Vipond, Douglas, 7
Vonnegut, Kurt, 89

Washburn, Paul, 24, 49–50, 57
Wasovwich, Bill, 63–64, 67

Waxham, Ethel, 115
Webb, Joseph M., 12
Weber, Ronald, 9, 11, 19–20, 78, 80
White, E.B., 8, 16
Whitman, Walt, 73
Winterowd, W. Ross, 13, 27, 110
Wolfe, Tom, 11, 13, 14, 17, 18
Wolff, Tobias, 18
Wooden, John, 44
Wordsworth, William, 15

Zavarzadeh, Mas'ud, 13
Zweig, Paul, 110

The Author

Michael Pearson is an Associate Professor of English at Old Dominion University in Norfolk, Virginia, where he teaches, both in the literature and the creative writing programs, courses in the American novel and workshops in creative nonfiction. He has written numerous essays and critical articles for a variety of journals, magazines, and newspapers, including the *Journal of American Culture, Mississippi Quarterly, The Southern Literary Journal*, the *New York Times*, the *Boston Globe*, and the *Atlanta Journal and Constitution*. He has published two works of nonfiction: *Imagined Places: Journeys into Literary America* (1991), which was listed by the *New York Times Book Review* as a Notable Book for 1992, and *A Place That's Known* (1994), a collection of interrelated essays. He has just completed a memoir, *Dreaming of Columbus: A Boyhood in the Bronx*, about growing up in New York City in the 1960s.

The Editor

Frank Day is a professor of English and head of the English Department at Clemson University. He is the author of *Sir William Empson: An Annotated Bibliography* (1984) and *Arthur Koestler: A Guide to Research* (1985). He was a Fulbright lecturer in American literature in Romania (1980–81) and in Bangladesh (1986–87).